I0125781

DECIDE to *Thrive*

Improving Business Performance through Decision Effectiveness

DECIDE to *Thrive*

Dr. Dale J. Albrecht
Dr. Maria Gomez Albrecht

Alonos®

© 2020

Copyright © 2020 by Alonos Corporation

Printed in the United States of America

All rights reserved. This book or any portion thereof may not be reproduced or used in any manner whatsoever without the express written permission of the publisher except for the use of brief quotations in a book review or scholarly journal.

First Printing: August 2020

ISBN-13: 978-1-948699-03-7 *(paperback)*

Alonos®
Dallas, Texas, United States of America

www.alonos.com

Alonos® is a registered trademark of the Alonos Corporation.

Special discounts are available on quantity purchases by corporations, associations, educators, educational institutions, and others. For details, contact the publisher.

Please contact Alonos® through our website or via email at:
information@alonos.com

Suggested bibliographical reference:

Albrecht, D.J. & Albrecht, M.G. (2020). *DECIDE to Thrive: Improving business performance through decision effectiveness*. Dallas, TX: Alonos Corporation.

$29.95
ISBN 978-1-948699-03-7
52995>

9 781948 699037

Contents

Figures

Tables

Examples

Authors

Dr. Dale J. Albrecht is CEO and Executive Partner for Alonos®. Alonos® is a consulting firm with products and services focused on business improvement, team improvement, and individual improvement. Alonos® provides a best-in-class employee survey product called Organizational Insights Check™ and a facilitated strategic planning workshop called Leadership Advance!® Dr. Albrecht is also an advisor and author for the Forbes Dallas Business Council and an Adjunct Professor for the University of Texas at Dallas.

Dr. Albrecht has fulfilled C-Suite leadership roles as Chief Human Resources and Risk Officer. Along with an extensive career in human resources, he has experience in general management, technical operations, and field engineering. Because of his early career experience in various business functions, Dr. Albrecht brings a holistic focus on business performance using systems thinking and multiple performance-based disciplines to drive performance improvement. Dr. Albrecht has worked in several industries including travel, retail, manufacturing, telecommunications, medical devices, construction, public safety, and Department of Defense.

Dr. Albrecht completed his Doctorate in Business Administration with Swiss Management Center University in Zug, Switzerland. He holds a Master of Business Administration from Columbia Southern University and a Bachelor of Science in Workforce Education & Development from Southern Illinois University, where he graduated Summa Cum Laude. He is also an appointed Six Sigma Master Black Belt. He also holds a certificate in Project Planning, Analysis and Control from George Washington University, and he is a Senior Certified Professional through the Society of Human Resource Management.

Dr. Maria Gomez Albrecht is an Executive Partner and Chief Marketing Officer for Alonos®. She specializes in multi-cultural applications of Alonos® products and services along with leading a multi-cultural client-based marketing agency.

Dr. Gomez Albrecht is an Adjunct Professor in Marketing at the University of Texas at Dallas for both the Executive MBA and the Global Leadership Executive MBA programs. She is also the Executive Vice President of Prospanica DFW, a non-profit organization established to empower and enable Hispanic professionals to achieve full academic potential, career advancement, and leadership skills.

Dr. Gomez Albrecht is an accomplished and highly-skilled business professional leveraging 25+ years of experience in several industries such as retail, medical, nonprofit, environmental, and education. Her specialties include strategic marketing, loyalty and growth programs, promotion and advertising campaign execution, brand and digital marketing, and new product launches in domestic and international markets. As a strategic *and* tactical thinker, she has extensive experience in ecommerce, sales operations, project management, data analytics, supply chain, and vendor management.

Dr. Gomez Albrecht completed her Doctorate in Business Administration at Swiss Management Center University in Zug, Switzerland. Her area of study, multicultural marketing in advertising and digital channels, is significant to understanding consumers' behaviors to maximize profits and build brand equity. She also has deep knowledge of multicultural marketing thanks to her fluency in Spanish and Portuguese, as well as business proficiency in French and Italian.

Preface

This book on decision effectiveness is part of a series of books that address the business performance disciplines. Our first book in the set was "Organizational Design *that* Sticks!" which was released in 2018. The book on organizational design was written first because, in our opinion, it is the one discipline that is most poorly applied and can have grave consequences on organizational culture. We chose to write this one next because decision effectiveness is one of the least understood disciplines shrouded in a lot of psychological "mystery."

We found that there are a lot of materials (e.g. books, podcasts, videos, e-courses, op-ed's, etc.) on the market that deal with the psychology of decision making. There's also much material on how to improve the quality of decision making from a personal and individual-leader standpoint; however, there are limited resources addressing decision making from a *business* standpoint. Most of the ones that are available are written to convince you that effective decision making is important. It's kind-of silly that these materials are as popular as they are…of course effective decision making is important! The question is: How do we get there? How do we get better as a team?

There is a gap when it comes to resources that both explain business decision making and how to work with teams to improve decision effectiveness. It was our goal to take the mystery out of the decision effectiveness discipline and turn it into practical application. This book along with the associated e-learning modules that our firm, Alonos®, produced will get you and your teams competent to start improving the effectiveness of your decision making in your business.

Introduction

This book on decision effectiveness is one of a set of books that addresses what are known as the seven business performance disciplines. Understanding and applying _all 7 disciplines_ in the right mix is what will enable you to achieve maximum success with your business goals and initiatives.

The use and application of the 7 disciplines is rooted in the foundations of systems thinking. Our businesses are systems. Our businesses exist within other systems such as economics, legal, and political. And, our businesses have sub-systems that exist within them. All of these systems operate in an interconnected manner; businesses do not operate in isolation. Change one thing in one place in your business and it will have implications to all the other interconnected parts of your business.

Unfortunately, many of us know and interact with our businesses in a "reduced" manner. We interact with our businesses as a _____ professional (fill in the blank.) If you're an operations person, you see your business through an operational lens. If you're a finance person, you see your business through a financial lens. If you're a product person, you see your business through a product lens. And, the list goes on. The higher up the corporate ladder you go in your career, the broader your view gets. An operations person who finally gets that executive promotion might suddenly have both operations and supply chain. Consequently, they now have to learn a new set of stocks and flows, constraints, and requirements…many of which they "battled" against as an operations person. Or, there's some turnover in the business and a senior level attorney gets promoted to lead both legal and human resources and picks up the title of Chief Administration Officer. Subsequently, s/he must now understand the people and organizational constraints that made those HR professionals so empathetic.

You can work your way up through the entire structure of any company, and the only person you will find who is chartered to care for a business as a *total system* is the Chief Executive Officer (CEO.) Even with CEO's, overwhelmingly, they come from functional roles and hardly none of them have a full business-systems-view in their background. From a systems capability standpoint, it would be quite reasonable to call this a bottleneck; we prefer to call it a pinch-point because *pinching* has an element of pain associated with it. This pinching, caused by a lack of a systems-view of our businesses, causes sub-optimization and incomplete attempts at driving initiatives and changes.

Of the 7 disciplines, decision effectiveness is the least understood, least practiced, and least leveraged. In director-level and above groups, we have found that less than 10% have any formal exposure, education, or experience with decision effectiveness. Below the director-level, that number drops to under 5%! Compared with the other disciplines, this is abysmal. But, let's fix that! Ready?!?

This book is going to walk you through a very logical approach to decision effectiveness. We'll start with the "business case" for decision effectiveness. The first few chapters examine the systems-dilemma that we just described, the 7 performance disciplines, and *why* decision effectiveness is important. If we're going to ask you to read a couple hundred pages, it makes sense that we would first explain *why* it's important. After this, the book goes into the "nuts and bolts" of decision effectiveness and how to improve it in your business. We stay completely focused on *improving* **business-decision-making**. This is a practical application-based book. This is not a book on psychology or academic frameworks. When this book is combined with our e-learning modules, you'll be able to begin the process of improving decision effectiveness on your key business decisions.

When decision effectiveness is bundled with the right mixture of the other six disciplines, you can achieve very high success rates. Among the 7 disciplines, decision effectiveness needs the most training, development, and attention. We hope you enjoy the book, learn some new skills, and are challenged to achieve greater success.

Our best in your endeavors toward improvement!

1. A Persistent Business Problem

Are you excited about the set of initiatives you have underway at your company? Do you feel good about the potential for growth and improved performance? Hate to break it to you, but research shows that *only 30% will succeed*.

Are you still excited?

The failure rates of business initiatives should get our attention. When we look at the research over the past 30 years, business initiative failure rates have averaged 66%!

Yes, a 66% failure rate.

We keep a record of successes and failures and regularly scrub research databases, search engines, case studies, books, opinion editorials, and many other sources. Admittedly, it is hard to find good quality *empirical* research on business projects and initiatives successes and failures. When you collect thousands of pieces of information, the macro trends are still obvious, and the conclusion is not good. Let's break it down a little further by type of initiative. The following are *failure rate* averages over 30 years by type of initiative:

- 66% - Information technology systems
- 72% - Organizational restructuring
- 67% - Business process redesign
- 71% - Pay incentives plans
- 52% - Software development
- 66% - All business initiative types combined

ERP Case Examples:

- In the first half of 2017 MillerCoors filed a $100M lawsuit against HCL over a breach of contract related to the implementation of their ERP software installation (Thibodeau, 2017). **$100M**

- In 2004 the U.S. Air Force embarked upon an ERP implementation that would replace over 200 outdated and disparate systems with an integrated and modern enterprise system. In 2013, it terminated the project after having spent $1.03 billion dollars (Kanaracus, 2013). **$1BN**

- In October of 2015, Select Comfort Corporation went live with a new ERP system. Initial announcements were all positive. Early 2017 earnings releases reported falling same store sales. ERP system issues were cited as contributing factors. The ERP project was stated to have been both behind schedule and over-budget (DePass, 2016).

It is worth noting that in software development the failure rates have improved 30% since the early 1990's, which is a significant improvement. If the trend in software development continues, by the mid 2020's failure rates will drop to around 30-40%, which would make it the only type of business initiative to have higher success rates than failure rates. All other types of business initiatives show no discernable trend of improvement.

Whenever we speak in front of groups about the failure rates of business initiatives, we encounter people who want to refute the numbers. Their counter-points are worth noting and discussing briefly. The largest counter-point is about conjecture versus empirical evidence. Yes, there's a large amount of conjecture out there especially in opinion editorials. However, there are also enough empirical research studies and case analyses to substantiate the failure rates. Our work with clients and our interactions with client employees also supports the failure statistics.

Another counter-point worth noting is around the definition of success. Astute business professionals are quick to point out that an accurate measurement of success or failure depends extensively on how one defines *success* at the outset. True. Take for example an information technology initiative to install a new Enterprise Resource Planning (ERP) system. These systems are complex. They include many functional modules, and often have requirements documents that are tens and even hundreds of pages long. This counter argument would suggest that if we achieve a subset of the requirements, the initiative should be counted as a partial success/failure based on the percentage of requirements achieved. The problem with this counter-argument is that it's a reductionist argument and avoids the business reality of embarking upon an ERP implementation. Let's explain.

Such an undertaking is often prefaced by a small number of business imperatives. One of our manufacturing clients undertook an ERP implementation initiative because they wanted to free up cash. The ERP system was supposed to provide them with better inventory management through improved *and* real-time inventory visibility from raw materials through to semi-finished and finished goods. Further, it was supposed to provide real-time visibility of finished goods in stock at various warehouses and in-transit to distribution centers and customers. With this improved inventory visibility, the company was going to be able to reduce inventory carrying levels throughout the supply chain, which would in-turn free up cash. The impact was 10's of millions of dollars per year. The ERP system requirements document was 189 pages long. The project was supposed to last 15-18 months. By the time the project was finished, 3.5 years had elapsed,

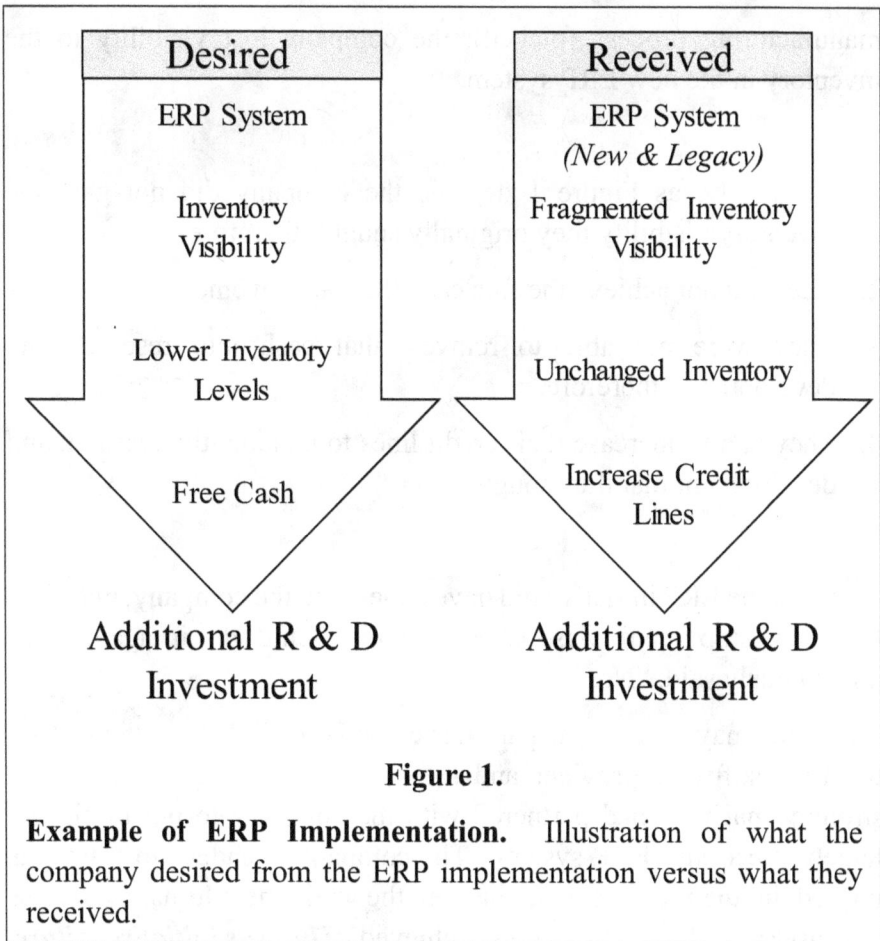

Figure 1.

Example of ERP Implementation. Illustration of what the company desired from the ERP implementation versus what they received.

which required 13 change orders, and the project had exceeded its original estimated budget by 275%. Along the way, the company had to de-scope 35% of their factories from the new ERP systems because they operated on a separate legacy system. These factories were part of an acquisition that was completed several years before the ERP initiative, but the de-scoping also meant that the associated traffic lanes, distribution, and warehousing also had to be de-scoped. They were able to do SKU rationalization and capture raw materials visibility for the company, but once the raw materials were released to the manufacturing process (picked), the company lost visibility to the inventory in the new ERP system.

1. Ultimately, as Figure 1 depicts, the company did not gain the inventory visibility they originally sought; therefore,

2. They did not achieve the free cash flow improvements; therefore,

3. They were not able to reinvest that cash into research and development; therefore,

4. They had to increase their credit lines to conduct the research and development that they sought.

Yes, the ERP initiative did have benefits to the company, but when the leadership team was asked if they would do it again, they unanimously said, "No."

Some may try to argue partial success/failure. As a matter of fact, the ERP software provider and the systems integrator both argued strongly that they had partnered with the company to put in place a hugely successful ERP system. The company's leadership team was unified in their assessment that, in the end, the ultimate business objective (freed up cash) was not achieved. *This was initiative failure*.

The empirical research studies that we have collected and studied follow the same approach to identifying and tracking root-criteria, and they produce the statistics presented at the opening of this chapter.

Another type of example, and one that all of us likely have experience with, is organizational structure change. Organizational efforts fair no better. Harvard Business Review reports "most studies still show a 60-70% failure rate for organizational change projects – a statistic that has stayed constant from the 1970's to the present" (Ashkenas, 2013). When that failure rate is extrapolated, it becomes daunting. According to the U.S. Census Bureau, in 2014 there were over 14,000 businesses in the United States that were large employers with 1,000 employees or more. These businesses represented an employed population of over 60M people. If you assume that every large business goes through some organizational change every year, and you factor-in the failure rates for organizational structure changes, it means that 42M people experience organizational change failures every year in the United States! Global data is much harder to come by, but Dunn and Bradstreet (2013) reported in 2013 that there were over 225M companies worldwide, across 200 countries. Applying similar assumptions and estimations, the number of people worldwide who experience organizational change failures every year is over 1.5 Billion!

Organization structure changes are unfortunately a "classic" example of failed business initiatives. It's common for companies to seek assistance with an organizational change that was conducted in the recent past, which they spent a lot of money to do, but it did not deliver the desired performance improvements. In many cases, the changes made things worse by damaging employee trust, culture, engagement, and productivity. In the worst of cases, companies embark upon a path of re-organizing over and over trying to achieve the performance improvements. *This is initiative failure.*

While some may want to argue for partial-success of business initiatives, if we are not getting the benefits originally put forward in our business cases, then the initiatives are failures. Business initiatives continue to fail at enormously high levels. Across the types of initiatives that we track, failure averages 66%! What you likely don't get a chance to read about is that we know how to fix this. We know how to turn this around.

2. Multi-Disciplinary Approach

Chapter Focus

There are disciplines that when combined, yield higher quality outcomes, faster execution, and generate improved sustainability. Business use of multi-disciplinary approaches lags other industries. When multi-disciplinary approaches are applied in business settings the success rates increase dramatically.

This chapter is a reprint and adaptation from
"Organizational Design that Sticks!"

Let's open with a short story from the fields of
construction and material sciences…

After years of wear-and-tear, your driveway needs to be redone. You believe that cement is a wonderful product that's durable and easy to maintain, so your goal is to contract to have a cement driveway installed. You get competitive bids, and you have one contractor tell you something that you didn't expect to hear:

"Cement is brittle and will fall apart quickly."

That's not what you had thought about cement, and the surprise on your face is evident, so the contractor explains:

"Cement by itself is very brittle and flaky. When put together with an aggregate material, it becomes stronger and stands up well under compression, which then makes it a good paving material. When mixed with an aggregate like gravel and sand, it becomes concrete."

Again, not the response you expected. I mean, come-on, they know what you're asking for right? Why the education in cement and concrete? You tell the contractor that you thought that cement and concrete were basically the same thing, and you get the courage to tell the contractor that you're a bit annoyed by the response:

"After all, you should understand that I fully intend to re-pave my driveway, and you should be quoting the right material to do so."

However, the next thing that the contractor tells you is also surprising, but this time you have a different reaction:

"I tell you this because the aggregate material that you select has a big impact on the durability and longevity of your driveway. Most of my competitors don't tell you this and don't allow you to choose. They quote what's convenient for them to quote, but that's often not what's best for the life of the pavement. For example, a washed aggregate is essential, meaning that the sand and stone needs to be free of chemicals and or other fine materials because they weaken the concrete. There are a lot of contractors out there that use dirty aggregate and the pavement falls apart after just a few years. Unfortunately, we see this a lot in driveways. Roadways are inspected with tight quality controls, but most customers doing driveways don't know this information and so they don't know to ask. I want you to have a quality experience both with me as your contractor and with your driveway. Also, we need to talk about rebar…"

You've just been given some valuable information regarding your driveway project; information that will determine the strength and longevity of the project. Your expression turns to one of interest, and you look on, waiting for him to continue:

"Most contractors will put in rebar. It's the third component that's needed for strong pavement that will last. Rebar is steel reinforcement, and it needs to be properly spaced along with a good aggregate and cement. If we do all that, you'll have a nice driveway for many years. We use spacers to keep the rebar at an equal distance above the base and centered in the concrete."

This story is an illustration of a material composite that we are all very familiar with. Steel-reinforced-concrete is all around us. It is the combination of materials (cement, aggregate, and steel) which gives it its strength and durability and makes it such a useful and versatile building material. Many things are built from this composite material: roadways, bridges, multi-story buildings, parking structures, and homes. Remove any one component, or try to skimp on any component, and you end up with a weak material that fails.

There are seven business disciplines that behave the same way. Use them together, and you will have strength in results and execution of your business initiatives. Consider this the business world's equivalent of material composites: a *multidisciplinary* and *ecosystems* approach. This approach *intentionally* blends disciplines together to improve the strength of business improvement efforts and their success rates. Much like material sciences, blending business disciplines improves the chances of success and reduces the risks of failure. The use of multidisciplinary approaches has been around for a while; however, the express use in a business context has been limited. Figure 2 shows recent publications that address the subject area from 2014 through 2017. Publication volume is an indicator of where research and application are being performed, and the numbers shown highlight the multi-disciplinary focus that has been placed on education, healthcare, and engineering. The right-hand bar shows that business is under-represented. The search for publications included a comprehensive query across popular-press, opinion-editorials, and scholarly research in the English language. While not globally comprehensive, it is representative of the lack of focus that's put on multi-disciplinary approaches in business, compared to other segments.

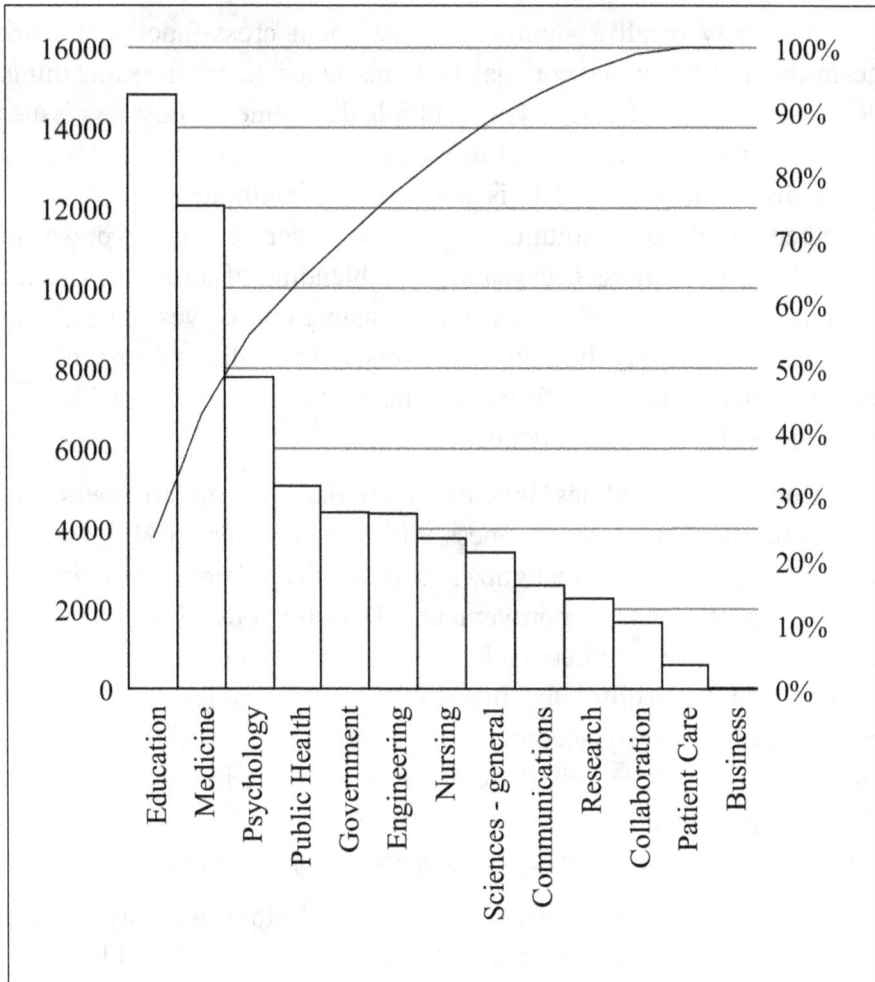

Figure 2

Multi-disciplinary Publications. The number of publications from 2014-2017 that are based on a multi-disciplinary approach, sorted by industry. Search terms were from a combination of results such as interdisciplinary, multi-disciplinary, and composites using a university library search engine that accesses 297 databases, 9,263 journals, and 39 subject guides. The same search on WorldCat yielded a similar result.

You may recall a significant buzz about cross-functional work teams in the 1990's, and you may be thinking that this is the same thing. Rest assured; it is not. Applying multiple disciplines to business issues is much more than the use of cross-functional work teams. Using a multi-disciplinary approach is about doing multiple *types of work* together, or blending solutions, in order to derive a more powerful impact on the business ecosystem. The blending of disciplines yields a strength in both *speed* and *quality* of business initiatives. The ability to intentionally apply the right mix of disciplines, allows companies to achieve their desired performance improvements more quickly and with higher levels of confidence.

Coupling disciplines together with decision effectiveness can boost the success rate of business initiatives to over 75%! A multi-disciplinary approach recognizes and applies systems thinking to business performance improvement. **Decision effectiveness** is one discipline of seven. Others include **organizational design**, **processes**, **systems**, **tools**, **people**, and **incentives**. True business performance improvement is rarely accomplished through the execution of a single discipline. It is also rarely done by driving change in only one part of the business; business improvement works in multiple areas to drive changes to the overall strategy and operation *of* the business.

An inverse lesson has also been learned along the way: Some types of activities should be avoided by themselves. Just like using cement by itself creates a brittle output, there are disciplines, that when used by themselves, create a brittle output. Decision effectiveness is one of them. Truth be told, each of the performance disciplines when implemented exclusively can yield a brittle and often bureaucratic outcome.

Another short story: It's the last few seconds of a basketball game, and the team is down by 1 point. Their star 3-point shooter is one more 3-point shot away from a personal record, and he has the ball. He puts out his best performance, making his way into shooting position, takes his record-shot, and misses. The team loses the game. The coaches are furious because they had two other players who were open and could have made a 2-point shot. Their star-shooter was thinking in a reductionist manner, and the coaches were thinking about the system. While this might be a simple illustration, the same kind of thinking occurs frequently in businesses. A functional leader proposes a project/initiative that makes a lot of sense for their operation. It has a good return on investment and would improve the efficiency of the unit. It gets approved. The changes are made. In the process of making the changes, it has a negative effect on another department, and the company risks losing capabilities, customers, revenue, and more. While good for the function, it has a negative impact on the company as a whole.

The best reason for engaging in systems thinking is because it correlates to improved performance (Skarzauskiene, 2010). Systems thinking competencies such as process orientation, systems logic, and understanding of mental models have the highest correlation to improved organizational performance. The strength of systems thinking makes a lot of sense. Our businesses exist within many contexts (e.g. socio, economic, geo-political, technical, etc.). Within our businesses we have systems within systems within systems; a concept called nesting. The larger the business the more complex the interactions. It is paramount to be able to evaluate the interrelations, comprehend the forces that are at work on the business, and subsequently choose changes that result in improved production both in the near-term and long-term.

Systems thinking is powerful through holistic evaluation of the nested components and how they interwork with each other, and it is the basis of Peter Senge's (2006) popular book. The approach is fundamentally different than a reductionist method of thinking. Reductionism is common in western societies. Reductionist-thinking breaks down a system into its component pieces and deals with each

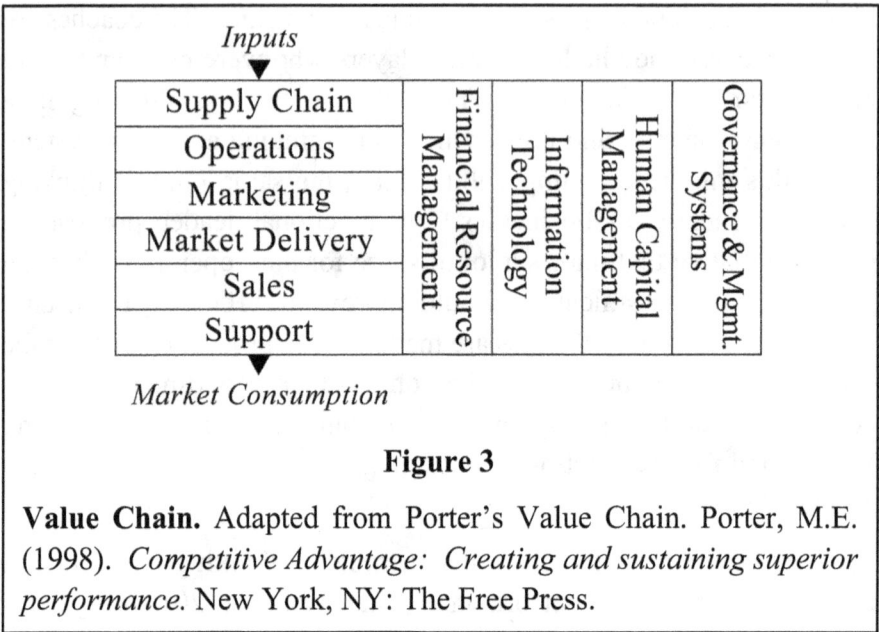

Inputs ▼	Financial Resource Management	Information Technology	Human Capital Management	Governance & Mgmt. Systems
Supply Chain				
Operations				
Marketing				
Market Delivery				
Sales				
Support				
▼ Market Consumption				

Figure 3

Value Chain. Adapted from Porter's Value Chain. Porter, M.E. (1998). *Competitive Advantage: Creating and sustaining superior performance.* New York, NY: The Free Press.

separately. One of the unfortunate outcomes of reductionist thinking is: what may be good for a sub-system might be bad for the larger system. The most powerful outcome of systems thinking is the sustained improvement of output in the company ecosystem, and this improvement is seen in both *efficiency* and *effectiveness*. Sustained improvements are accomplished by *intentional* and *planned* selection/adjustment of *multiple variables* across *multiple disciplines*.

Figure 3 shows a depiction of a value chain, which is useful in visualizing companies as systems. All companies and organizations transform inputs into products and/or services which are consumed in the marketplace. There are direct value chain functions, which are shown on the left. These are called direct functions because they directly "touch" the inputs in the conversion. There are also indirect value chain functions, which are shown on the right. These are called indirect functions because they indirectly affect the inputs in the conversion and more-often focus on enabling the direct functions. In today's business-world it would be reasonable to adapt Porter's value

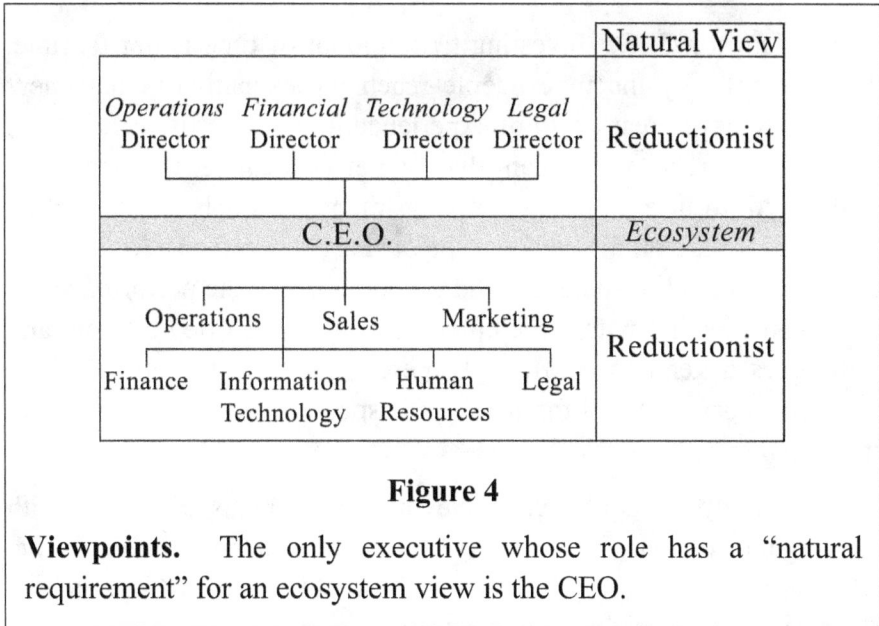

	Natural View
Operations Financial Technology Legal Director Director Director Director	Reductionist
C.E.O.	*Ecosystem*
Operations Sales Marketing Finance Information Human Legal Technology Resources	Reductionist

Figure 4

Viewpoints. The only executive whose role has a "natural requirement" for an ecosystem view is the CEO.

chain to show information technology as *direct* or *indirect*, depending on the company's products and services..

Systems thinking is also one of those things that seems to be easier said than done. Corporate career progression doesn't naturally support the development of systems thinking. Even ideal executive management teams struggle with systems thinking. The reason that teams struggle with systems thinking is that most people receive a limited breadth of *functional* experience through their careers. Even when development and career growth is planned and intentional, people will get exposure to two or three or four functional areas. That exposure is fantastic, but it still does not cover the whole of a business ecosystem. To have experienced the ecosystem of a single business, one would have to cover 10 value chain functions (Figure 3) How long would you have to work in a value chain function to understand that function with a moderate degree of expertise? A few years? So, if you aspired to the CEO position and you wanted to work 3 years in each value chain function, you would have to invest 30 years prior to being a candidate for CEO. Investing that amount of time is not feasible. Consequently, by the time people reach the executive management level, they have great depth of experience in a few of the value chain areas, but rarely more than that. Yet, executive managers are challenged to use systems thinking mental models so that their contributions are on the *whole* of the *business ecosystem*. At the same time, they are still responsible and accountable for the performance of their own function within the enterprise. There is often tension, and sometimes a genuine conflict of interest, between the needs of the business ecosystem and the needs of a specific value chain function. It's a challenge to say the least.

Inevitably, the <u>only</u> executive manager who is *chartered* with viewing the company in its totality, as a system, is the Chief Executive Officer (CEO) (Figure 4.) Beyond the CEO, the only other people chartered to view the company as a total system is the Board. Even here though, selection criteria hinder systems thinking at the board-level as much as it does with executive management. Boards often look for directors who have deep expertise in functional specialties like accounting, information technology, operations, legal, and marketing/sales. Reductionist thinking is one of the biggest barriers to systems thinking, for both CEO's and board members. They almost always have depth of expertise in only a few functional areas.

There are seven disciplines that are primary drivers of ecosystem performance changes. Each is used as a change-lever and impacts how the system operates; adjusting any of them will change the business ecosystem performance.

Those disciplines are:

1. Organizational Structure
2. Decisioning
3. Process Design
4. Systems
5. Tools
6. People
7. Incentives

Decisioning is *one* of the seven performance change levers. As stated in a previous chapter, 66% of business initiatives fail. From experience, one of the most common causes of failure is that these disciplines are applied as "one-discipline engagements." For example, management works hard at coming up with what is believed to be the next-best way to structure the organization; the structure is implemented, and then performance is expected to get better. No one addresses the decision rights, processes, systems, tools, people, or incentives. A few weeks or months later the performance is still suffering, and so management goes after another change...maybe this time replacing the leader (people.) Then, a few months later when that doesn't work, management goes after an even larger organizational change. It becomes a cycle of restructuring that doesn't deliver performance improvements. What needs to be realized is that every one of the disciplines is *interdependent* with the other six.

- The organizational structure defines and *implies* roles, responsibilities, authority levels, and workflow. The organizational chart is a method of communication, to the company, about each of these.
- If changes are made on an **organizational** chart, but **decision/authority rights** are not defined and communicated, the company will end up with people in roles who cannot effectively execute the duties of their jobs as intended.

- If work **processes** aren't changed to match, the people in the new structure are left guessing about what changes in work activities management really wanted from them…who knows what kind of workflow changes will be gained, if any.
- If **systems** requirements and changes aren't defined to match the new organizational structure, any automated workflow, approvals, and movement of information won't occur; thereby, it would have the effect of crippling the intended authority levels and decision effectiveness of the roles.
- Avoid the consideration of **tools**, and people will not be able to fulfill what was a well-intended design (e.g. If a new leadership role is not enabled with the right reports and analytics, the decision quality will suffer.)
- Put in place a great organizational structure, put **people** in roles that aren't a good fit for them, and performance will often drop precipitously along with the unintended development of negative team dynamics.
- Some would go so far as to say, 'if you put in place the right **incentives**, the rest of it will fall in place.' Without a doubt, the right incentive design is crucial for motivating both work activities and performance outcomes, but incentives work in conjunction with organizational structure and the other disciplines.

Changes in any one of the disciplines will always carry subsequent changes in the others. Successful execution of business performance improvements requires a multidisciplinary approach. Only a multi-disciplinary approach can deliver analyses that properly diagnose a performance problem. Only a multi-disciplinary approach will generate a change proposal that will improve the organizational ecosystem in total.

3. Why Decision Effectiveness is Important

Chapter Focus

Decision effectiveness is the least understood discipline of the seven; therefore, it presents the most opportunity for improvement. Decision effectiveness has been proven to directly affect a company's financial performance and culture. It is a critical component of leadership and can bring objectivity to an organization's unwritten power structures.

Before we go too much further, it's beneficial to spend a little time understanding *WHY*. Why should we care about decisioning? We all make a lot of decisions every day, from what shoes do we wear to major investments for the future of our companies. The vast majority of our decisions are made intuitively, but our most important decisions should be made with reasoned thought, participation of others, and deliberate choice. There are legitimate and proven reasons why we should focus on decisioning, which includes its ability to drive business performance.

Financial Performance

Research that has been conducted in decision effectiveness has examined the correlation with financial performance. There are business books that have been published by consulting firms highlighting the impact of decision effectiveness on financial performance. Unfortunately, the same firms keep the data out of view, so it is impossible to verify the claims; this is understandable because they're reporting against their own customer base. That customer base surely has confidentiality requirements. There have been several scholarly research projects conducted on the same subject. The data produced by these research projects are a better reference point because their results follow peer-reviewed empirical research guidelines and the content of the studies are publicly available so they can be verified.

One such study was conducted by Carmeli, Sheaffer, & Halevi in 2008. They tested three hypotheses, which are summarized as:

1. Are group decision methods positively correlated to decision effectiveness?
2. Is there a positive correlation between decision effectiveness and business performance?
3. How much does decision quality impact business performance?

Their findings on the second hypothesis are powerful. To discern performance, they measured four financial metrics, including:

- Return on Sales (ROS)
- Return on Assets (ROA)
- Return on Equity (ROE)
- Market Share

Shown in Table 1, decision effectiveness has a slight positive correlation to business performance in each of the metrics listed above. Group participation in strategic decisions also has a slight positive correlation to business performance. When all data is reviewed and regression analyses are completed, the researchers report that "a positive and significant relationship between decision effectiveness and organizational performance" exists at a correlation of .0.51. In the realm of statistics this is considered a *moderate* positive correlation. In business, this is a powerful correlation.

	Decision Effectiveness	Group Participation
Return on Sales	0.16	0.19
Return on Assets	0.21	0.20
Return on Equity	0.24	0.17
Market Share	0.30	0.13

Table 1

Financial Impact. Adapted from Carmeli, Sheaffer, & Halevi (2008): *Does participatory decision-making in top management teams enhance decision effectiveness and firm performance?* Illustrating the positive correlation of decision effectiveness practices on financial performance.

Other research has been conducted which demonstrates similar correlations to performance. In a research study conducted by Elbanna and Child (2007) and published in the Strategic Management Journal, they showed a *moderate* positive correlation between company performance and rational decision making. Rational decision making is the application of formal thought processes to assess facts and alternatives. Rational decision making was contrasted with other methods such as *intuitive* decision making and *politically-driven* decision making. The correlation score given in this study between rational decision making and performance was 0.54 (p.442). In the realm of statistics, a 0.54 correlation coefficient is considered a *moderate* correlation. The strongest correlation would be -/+ 1.0. We wouldn't expect a correlation of 1.0 with any of the seven disciplines, but for a single discipline to have a 0.54 positive correlation is *significant* and definitely worth giving attention.

Examining correlation coefficients emphasizes the point of the previous chapter: <u>making real improvements requires a multidisciplinary approach</u>. When you combine the disciplines and use them to work on the business ecosystem together, you are getting additional leverage from each of those discipline's positive correlations. It would be a stretch to claim a mathematical or statistical lift from bundling, because empirical research has not been conducted to demonstrate such an effect. However, it would stand to reason (and worth testing) that bundling them together is accretive to improving performance. This matches with our experience working with many clients and initiatives over the years: bundling the right mix of disciplines makes sense and yields *optimal performance improvement*.

A word on the topic of **innovation** as it relates to decision effectiveness: If your financial performance is dependent on *innovation,* then you need to be even more concerned with decision effectiveness. Innovation is directly dependent on decision effectiveness. An article by Larson (2018) describes what an organization needs in order to have high levels of innovation. Some of these practices include empowerment, productive conflict, broad-based inputs, speed of decision making, effort-efficiency, clear communications, and aligned execution. All practices mentioned in the article are decision-making practices. Innovation thrives on effective decision making.

Cultural Impact

Culture as an overall construct is very complex and multi-faceted, but without a doubt decision making processes have a determinant and measurable impact on a company's culture. Through the decision-making process that leaders facilitate, they establish a *part* of the organization's culture.

Authority		Accountability	
		Low	High
High		Too many initiatives Resource inefficiencies Lack of alignment Unclear vision	Empowered leaders High level of trust Forward progress
Low		Stalled efforts Disengaged workforce Negative outlook Wasted effort	High frustration Slow execution Indecision & re-decision

Figure 5

Cultural Impact. Matrix depicting the impact of decisioning characteristics of authority and accountability on cultural dynamics.

Let's first look at the cultural impact of effective decisioning. Refer to Figure 5. An *effective* decision-making process places decisions at the *right place* in the organization and establishes a high level of both **authority** and **accountability**. When decisions, along with supporting roles, are identified and assigned to fit the business environment it generates positive cultural implications. As the top-right quadrant of Figure 5 depicts, this generates empowerment and trust, and it propels the organizational forward.

Looking at the top-left quadrant in Figure 5, if we drive high levels of authority and low accountability, we end up with too many initiatives, resource inefficiencies, lack of alignment, and unclear vision. If you stop and think about this, it makes sense. If our leaders are all thinking that they each own decision making and there's little accountability, then they will do what they believe is best for their respective organizations. This will put the company in a position where the various organizational units are vying for resources internally, especially from indirect and support groups. The general impression by the working groups is that everything is a priority, and when everything is a priority, nothing is a priority.

Looking at the bottom-right of Figure 5, if we do the opposite of the previous paragraph and drive high levels of accountability and low authority, we end up with very different cultural implications. This generates high frustration, slow execution, and promotes both indecision and re-decision. This one makes sense when we think about it too. If the leaders of a company are all held highly accountable, but very few people are able to make a decision, it generates a bottleneck. That bottleneck slows decisioning down dramatically. When someone tries to make a decision, it gets questioned, reviewed, escalated, and overruled. Culturally, this is a very slow moving and frustrating organization.

It can get worse than the previous two paragraphs describe; look at the bottom-left quadrant of Figure 5. If we have low levels of both authority and accountability, the cultural impacts are indeed quite negative. If there is little decision-making authority and role clarity, and there's also little accountability, the results are apathetic. Employees will experience a culture of stalled efforts, disengagement, negativity, and wasted effort.

The cultural impacts of effective decision making are dramatic. By being intentional about where and with whom key decisions are placed in the organization, we drive higher levels of both authority and accountability, which in-turn improves decision effectiveness. We can drive empowerment through proper placement of both decision-making and the roles that participate in the decisioning processes (which we will review in later chapters.)

Part of Effective Leadership

Another reason why decision effectiveness is important is that it is an integral part of being an effective leader. Many publications have been written about how to improve your own decision making, often having a strong orientation to self-improvement and self-development. When it comes to being successful in a *business* leadership role, where you are leading teams of people to achieve combined success, decision making is a group and organizational process that requires intentional thought, consideration, and design. Consider this popular quote by author John C. Maxwell:

> Inability to make decisions is one of the principal reasons executives fail. Deficiency in decision making ranks much higher than lack of specific knowledge or technical know-how as an indicator of leadership failure.

What Mr. Maxwell is pointing out here is relevant and true. Making decisions is one thing but making decisions that are effective and *team-oriented* is more intricate. It's both easy and common to point back to the executive and say that their decision-making was flawed, but the reality of our businesses is that decision-making is a *team effort*. Executives don't make decisions in a vacuum (usually); they are reacting to input and recommendations from other experts both internally and externally. This being the case, the point of leadership failure is team cohesiveness and trust, and whether or not a team can participate in productive conflict and arrive at informed choices. This team dynamic is emphasized by the motivational speaker and former Navy SEAL Brent Gleeson:

> Good leaders surround themselves with trusted advisors and subject matter experts, so that they can access a constant flow of data to make better decisions (2012).

Team cohesiveness and trust enables empowerment and drives high levels of both authority and accountability. When leaders foster these characteristics in the decision-making process, they put themselves in a position where they, as individual leaders, make few decisions. In other words, delegation is part of the culture. That's Peter Drucker's point: Effective executives do not make a great many decisions. They concentrate on what is important (1967 & 1993).

Notice the date-stamp on Peter Drucker's quote; that one goes back to January of 1967. We've known the tenets of effective decision making in business for decades. This last point is that effective leaders focus on a few critical decisions. If we have the cultural dynamics that we want, the *team* engages in distributed decision making.

Least Understood

This last reason will serve as a book-end for this chapter, complimenting the first reason. With a strong correlation to financial performance, decision effectiveness is the *least understood* of the 7 performance disciplines. Less than 10% of the workforce has any kind of formal experience or exposure to decision effectiveness.

Last year alone, our firm produced training that reached over 1,000 business professionals, at the director-level and up, on 5 continents. When we poll/survey participants we consistently find a low percentage of people who have experience with decision effectiveness.

Based on our interactions, below are the percentages of people who have formal exposure to each of the seven disciplines. Decision effectiveness is the lowest; the other 6 disciplines put up much higher numbers:

75% - Organizational structure and design
80% - Process design
50% - Systems and work automation
90% - Job Tools
85% - People (Learning & Development, Talent Management)
60% - Incentives
07% - Decision effectiveness

Keep in mind that these response rates were for a *global* group of directors and up. When working with people below the director-level, all of the rates drop precipitously. At the manager-level, our experience is that they all drop 10-15 percentage points, and decision effectiveness drops to less than a 3% experience rate. It is easy to conclude that our collective understanding and mastery of decision effectiveness is in crisis in the business world.

Summary

Decision effectiveness is a vitally important discipline for driving business performance improvement. It has a positive correlation to improved financial performance in revenue growth, profitability, and shareholder return. The cultural impacts of poor decision-making processes are undeniable, and the positive elements of high authority and accountability clearly springboard off of team cohesiveness, trust, productive conflict, and collaboration. When we look across our leaders and our teams, there is a gap in our knowledge. We need to boost our mastery of this discipline and use it in conjunction with the other six performance disciplines to achieve the success rates that we desire.

4. What is Decision Effectiveness?

> **Chapter Focus**
>
> This is essentially a "definitions" chapter, establishing a foundational understanding for what decision effectiveness is in a business setting. This chapter examines what we can expect from improvement efforts in decisioning. We look at who is impacted by our decision making and the various dimensions of measuring effectiveness.

Now that we understand *why* decision effectiveness is important, let's spend a little time defining the concept of *effectiveness* when it comes to "landing a decision" for a business. There are several schools-of-thought, models, and frameworks related to decision rights, and we'll look at a few of those in a subsequent chapter on "decision and process methods." To establish the groundwork, let's look at the constructs of effectiveness in business decision-making.

Decision Making

In the most-simple sense, decision-making is *making a choice*. Sometimes we make choices *intuitively* and sometimes we make choices through *intentional reasoning*. We make decisions (choices) all day everyday both in our personal and business lives. For the purposes of this book we are focusing on business decisions.

There is some psychology behind decisioning. While this is not intended to be a book on the psychology of decision making, it is useful

TH15 M3554G3 53RV35 TO PR0V3
H0W 0UR M1ND5 C4N D0 4M4Z1NG
TH1NG5! 1MPR3551V3 TH1NG5!
YOUR M1ND 4UT0M4T1C4LLY
P70C3S53S 1T W1TH OUT 3V3N
TH1NK1NG 4B0UT 1T…5Y5T3M 1!

Tehn trehe is fplinipg lrtetes anruod,
ahd it h6s tne smam efecft. Y0u c6n
raed it jsut as qckuliy bcaesue yuor
ssyetm o1e tnihnikg uess ptteanrs to
raed lugagnae.

Figure 6

Language Processing. A linguistic alteration to illustrate how you process language in patterns versus reading each letter independently.

to have some of the context as we define decision making in business. There are a couple items, coming out of the field of psychology, that resonate for us as business leaders trying to drive change and improvement within our organizations.

Psychology tells us that as human beings we have two fundamental systems of thinking (Kahneman, 2011). Very creatively known as System 1 and System 2. System 1 thinking is our thinking process that is automatic and leverages pattern-recognition. Because of this, it requires a relatively lower amount of effort and we have a large capacity for this type of thinking. The language center of our brain uses system 1 thinking and it's the reason that you can easily read Figure 6. If the first and last letter of a word are close to accurate, and the number of characters is accurate, your brain reads the word as-if it were correctly spelled. The second paragraph in Figure 6 flips the letters around inside each word, just to make it a little more challenging, and you can still read this paragraph just as fast as the first paragraph. This phenomenon is true in every language. These little puzzles float around social media all the time with headings like, "Only the smartest 2% can read this." Sorry to burst your bubble, but it has nothing to do with how smart you are. Everyone on the planet uses the same "pattern-recognition engine" to process language. You might still be super-smart, but it's not only because you can read Figure 6.

System 2 thinking is our thinking process that is conscious and requires focused energy and effort. This thinking process enables logic, analysis, and reasoning, and it allows us to deal with abstract and complex information. It is accurate and reliable. The mere use of System 2 thinking is a choice; it is a choice to focus and process by following a set of steps that yield rational thoughts and conclusions. In order for System 2 to perform well, you must be able to focus and operate without interrupting the thought processes; interruptions will compromise the quality, speed, effort, and the output itself.

In research conducted by Psychology Today, it was estimated that a human being makes an average of 35,000 decisions per day (Guttman, 2019). Now, that's everything from "What shoes do I wear?" to "Do I invest two million in this project?" That's a lot of decisions every day. Because of this high volume of decisions, we need System 1 thinking to be productive. And, that's Kahneman's point of view when he calls System 1 thinking the 'star of the show' (2011). Without System 1 thinking we could not function well in our world.

Extending this psychology basis into our businesses and organizations: since our business organizations are comprised of people, it stands to reason that our organizations exhibit aspects of System 1 and System 2 thinking. If you've ever been part of a decision that went something like this, "We're going to do it this way because we've always done it this way"… that's an aspect of System 1 thinking at an organizational level. "We're going to do it this way because we've always done it this way" means that it's worked well in the past, we're using pattern recognition, and we're going to render the same decision because it requires a low amount of effort and energy. With the many thousands of decisions that we make every day, both individually and organizationally, we need System 1 thinking. But, when we want to *change* how a decision is made in our businesses, we need to invoke System 2 thinking in order to "re-wire" the organization.

We're asking people to change *how* they make a decision. Doing so means that we are asking people, and entire organizations, to stop, use System 2 thinking, and to intentionally change how they work. This requires effort. This is how we build new organizational muscle-memory. It requires a new conscious effort at first. With practice it becomes easier. Over time, it becomes automatic and it then emerges as the new System 1 pattern. So, realize going in that there is a psychological aspect to modifying decision-making in a business, and that the changes will take time to become the "new normal." These decision-making psychological elements are important to understand when seeking to improve decision effectiveness.

Example: The Entrepreneur's Trap

It is in the context of System 1 and System 2 thinking that a significant portion of the "Entrepreneur's Trap" is rooted.

The essence of this trap is that an entrepreneur finds it difficult, if not impossible, to change their ways as their business grows and develops. The inability to change means that eventually the business outgrows its creator, the entrepreneur, and they become a barrier to the ongoing growth and development of the business.

The entrepreneur suffers from being stuck in a system 1 thinking pattern. They execute decision-routines automatically because they have spent years doing so. What makes it even more difficult for an entrepreneur to apply System 2 thinking, is that they have enjoyed success along the way. The growth and success of the business was based on the entrepreneur's decisions.

To be told that you have to change the decision making that made you successful, just doesn't seem rationale.

The entrepreneur's trap is an example and another reason why the discipline of decision effectiveness is so valuable. The ability to identify key business decisions, how they function today, and what's needed in the future, is unique to this discipline. *Decision Effectiveness* is the only discipline that can illustrate how the future growth of the business is dependent upon key decisions, team efforts, and role clarity.

Defining Decision Effectiveness

Determining whether a business decision is effective or not requires examining the outcome of any given decision. Decision outcomes are often measured borrowing from what's known as the Theory of Triple Constraints (Wyngaard, Pretorius, & Pretorius, 2012). This theory is commonly applied to the profession of project management, and it juxtapositions the three dimensions of *quality*, *speed*, and *cost* to be interdependent with one another. In some of the more recent publications on decision effectiveness, the theory of triple constraints was expanded, and some of the language adjusted, to include *quality*, *speed*, *yield*, and *effort*. In the decision effectiveness research, the word *effort* replaces the word *cost*. In our practice we

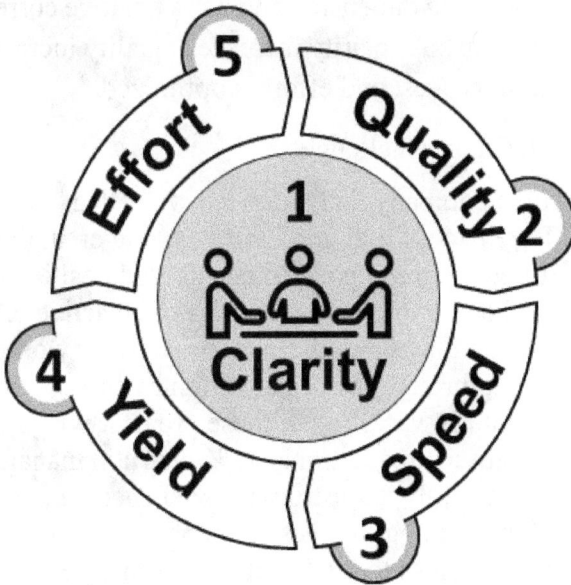

Figure 7

Dimensions of Decision Effectiveness. These 5 dimensions of effective decisions are interdependent.

expand on this further and add a critical *fifth* dimension which we have found <u>must</u> be present to drive improvements in decision effectiveness. This fifth dimension is *clarity,* or more specifically *role clarity.* Let's walk through each of these dimensions shown in Figure 7, and we'll illustrate how the concept of interdependent constraints plays out in each.

The first dimension of decision effectiveness, shown in Figure 7, is *clarity.* This is the leading dimension, which is why it is depicted in the center of the figure. Role clarity is of paramount importance when improving decision effectiveness. If people are not familiar with the role types, how to perform them, and what their own assignments are, it is nearly impossible to achieve improved decision effectiveness.

Clarity is a key *enabling* dimension and has a positive correlation to the other four dimensions. As clarity increases, quality increases, speed is optimized, yield improves, and effort is optimized.

Example: Good Churn Challenges

We worked with a company that had what we called "good churn challenges." They had several good things going on in their business, but ironically these good things caused positional churn. The company had one of the best examples of an active talent development program in place, and they proactively worked on the movement of talent through the organization as part of a person's career development. It was through these proactive development moves that they caused an additional 15% churn in manager and director position. Luckily, their true turnover (people leaving the company) was low, coming in at less than 5% per year. Combined, positional churn was close to 20%, but, again, the greatest part of this was good and desirable.

We picked up this company as a customer doing work around employee engagement. We rolled out an employee survey, which measures decision effectiveness along with engagement, culture, and performance disciplines. As we measured decision effectiveness from period-to-period, we noticed the scores bouncing around without any discernable pattern.

Working with the customer to try to understand this, we learned about their active talent management approach. And, it was this approach that was causing their metrics to bounce around erratically. What was happening was…as they moved leaders in an out of roles, it took them time to learn work processes, organizational structure, and the unwritten cultural elements of how things were done and how decisions were made. As people moved around, this "institutional knowledge" went with them, and the next person to assume a leadership role had to re-learn all the unwritten elements of the job all over again. The learning and re-learning caused their metrics to jump up and down in the departments and functions where they had active talent movement.

The challenge was more than a metric though. The metric is a reflection of how the organization made decisions. Erratic metrics on decision effectiveness meant that management decision-making was under pressure. Sometimes decisions were made well, and other times they were not. It needed to be stabilized so that the good work the company was doing around talent development didn't have this negative effect on business performance.

By implementing the decision effectiveness discipline, we were able to provide sustainable improvements. It started by identifying and defining key decisions, followed by the clear assignment of roles in the decision-making process. Role clarity was a profound enabler for the company because it meant that everyone in the organization understood what was expected of them and how they participated. Consequently, as the leaders were moved around, they landed in departments where everyone was already fully aware of their own expectations, and it became a team effort to rally around the newly assigned leader. Key decisions and roles became part of the on-boarding process. The work around decision effectiveness dramatically improved successful leadership transitioning and shortened time to productivity from 18-24 months down to 30-45 days!

The second dimension of decision effectiveness is the *perceived quality* of a decision. One of the most cited works on quality was written by David Garvin in 1987 and published by the Harvard Business Review. In this article Mr. Garvin outlines eight aspects of *product* quality including 1) performance, 2) features, 3) reliability, 4) conformance, 5) durability, 6) serviceability, 7) aesthetics, and 8) perception. Several of these categories do not apply to decisioning because we're not working with products per se. There are a couple aspects that do have parallel use such as performance and reliability. These two aspects are called-out separately in the decisioning dimensions in Figure 7 as yield and effort. For the purposes of evaluating and understanding decisioning, quality of decision making addresses the eighth aspect in Garvin's model, which is *perceived quality*. A decision is viewed and perceived from *hindsight*, answering questions such as:

- Did we make a good quality decision?
- All things considered at the time, was the decision sufficiently vetted and did we perform our due diligence before making the choice?

Viewing the quality dimension with constraints, it is interdependent on speed, yield, effort, and clarity. If we want to drive a higher quality decision, we will need *clarity* on roles in the decisioning process. We may need to *slow* down and put more *effort* into the decisioning process. And, achieving a higher quality decision should mean that the *yield* (output) will better match our estimates contained within business cases that have been developed.

The third dimension of decision effectiveness is *speed*. It's common for people to think that *faster is better*, but that is not what's meant by this dimension. Faster isn't always better. There is a concept known as the "Second-Mover Advantage" (Carpenter, 2013). The reality of this concept been around for a very long time, but Gregory Carpenter does a nice job of summarizing it in his 'primer' published with the Kellogg School of Management at Northwestern University. One very telling quote is, "that pioneers [first-to-market] were more successful than late movers in just 15 of 50 product categories" (p. 1). Think about that for a minute. That means that second-to-market/second-movers (or later) had an advantage in 70% of the product categories!

Of course, it also means that if your business produces products in the 30% where first-to-market really does matter, then speed is of the essence. But, for the vast majority of us, we don't need to push to be first. As a matter of fact, slowing down can make a big difference when it comes to decision quality, which we mentioned in the previous paragraph. Slowing down allows us to do some things better, such as listening to customers and employees, collecting broader input and ideas, ensuring collaboration, and building more thorough business cases. An effective decision is one that is made at a *pace* that is *right for your business*. From a constraints standpoint speeding up or slowing down directly impacts quality, yield, effort, and role clarity.

The fourth dimension of decision effectiveness is *yield* or outcome. This dimension of decision effectiveness is also one that is viewed in hindsight and answers the question:

- Did we get the outcome that we thought we would get when we built the business case and made the decision?

Yield functions in a lot of ways like an after-action-review, and an *effective* decision *generates an outcome that we expected*. When we go through the process of collecting inputs, doing analyses, making recommendations, and ultimately making decisions, we have expectations. These expectations can take many forms such as revenue, profit, market share, customer satisfaction, customer retention, product sales volume, and many others. These are all examples of outcomes and yield. From a constraints standpoint improving yield typically means that we need to improve quality, achieve the right speed, apply the right effort, and ensure that we have role clarity in the organization.

The fifth dimension of decision effectiveness is *effort*. This dimension isn't necessarily about *more* or *less*, it's all about the *right* amount of effort. Applying more effort doesn't necessarily improve decision effectiveness. Effort is the one dimension of decisioning that looks at decision *efficiency* specifically. The desire in any business is to be as efficient as possible while not compromising quality, speed, yield, or clarity. From a constraints standpoint, effort is the most lagging of the dimensions. This is also why we list it fifth. But, effort is also the most dependent on role clarity. The better we are at decision effectiveness organizationally, the less effort (resources) we will need to invest to get the quality, speed, and yield that we desire.

An effective business decision process has all five dimensions in place:

1. We have **Clarity** of roles
2. We are confident in **Quality**
3. We are able to work at optimal **Speed**
4. The **Yield** and outcomes are what we expected
5. The **Level of Effort** applied to decision making is optimal

Each of these dimensions are interdependent with the others and improving decision effectiveness requires a holistic eco-system approach.

Decision Rights

When we examine *decision rights* as a construct, it's important to note that we are considering team-oriented decisioning. More will be discussed in subsequent chapters on various models of decision-making ranging from individual through team-based and consensus-based. As a definition, *decision rights* establish role types, role assignments, role authority, and role autonomy. Decision rights are the *clarity* dimension in the previous paragraphs. To improve *clarity*, one must work on decision rights for each key decision in an organization. And, it addresses much more than just "who makes the decision."

Let's say that you're the Chief Financial Officer for a company, and there's a situation developing where you've learned that one of your company's largest customers has become insolvent. You have to make a decision about, "What new credit terms you're willing to extend to this customer." Now, you get to choose how you would like to learn of this new information:

A. Your leader of Accounts Receivables comes to you and says, "We've got an issue with our biggest customer. They're delinquent for over a quarter, and I've just learned that they're having solvency problems. What should we do?"

-or-

B. Your leader of Accounts Receivables comes to you and says, "We've got an issue with our biggest customer. They're delinquent for over a quarter, and I've just learned that they're having solvency problems." I got together with the account leaders for both our company and theirs and we talked about what's going on. We came up with three alternatives that I'd like to run by you, and I have a recommendation for how we can move forward. By the way, I've already run these past legal and they're on-board with all three alternatives. Can I review these with you and make a recommendation?"

As the CFO, you're the decider, but would you like your employee to take approach A or B? Most of us would prefer approach B by leaps and bounds! Approach B is exactly what clarity and decision rights is all about...it's about *who* fulfills which *roles* in *each critical decision*. We will examine decision rights in much more detail in subsequent chapters.

Controlling Variable	Quality	Speed	Yield	Effort	Clarity
Quality ↑		↓	↑	↑	↑
Quality ↓		↑	↓	↓	↓
Speed ↑	↓		↓	↑	↓
Speed ↓	↑		↑	↓	↑
Yield ↑	↑	↓		↑	↑
Yield ↓	↓	↑		↓	↓
Effort ↑	?	?	?		?
Effort ↓	?	?	?		?
Clarity ↑	↑	↑	↑	↓	
Clarity ↓	↓	↓	↓	↑	

Table 2

Dimension Relationships. Identifies the typical relationships between the dimensions of decision effectiveness.

> **Quality** typically has an inverse relationship with *speed* and a similar relationship with *yield* and *effort*.

> **Speed** typically has an inverse relationship with *quality*, *yield*, and *clarity* and a similar relationship with *effort*.

> **Yield** typically has an inverse relationship with *speed* and a similar relationship with *quality*, *effort*, and *clarity*.

> **Effort** is a unique dimension because increasing or decreasing effort, as a controlling variable, does not predictably *generate* changes in the other dimensions.

> **Clarity** is at the center of Figure 6 because it is central to all of the other dimensions. Increases in role clarity typically generate improvements in all of the other four dimensions.

Summary

Making effective decisions in business involves several components. Table 2 shows the interrelationships between these dimensions. There is a psychological component that we need to understand because our organizations are comprised of people. The psychology of how *we think* is intricately tied to how *organizations think* and render decision making.

If we want to drive improvements in decision effectiveness, we need to focus on the five key dimensions of:

1. Clarity

2. Quality

3. Speed

4. Yield

5. Effort

Clarity must come first because without role clarity it is nearly impossible to improve the other four dimensions, and that is where decision rights come into play. Decision rights are how we establish role types, assign roles, and empower our people.

5. Hidden Matters

Chapter Focus

This chapter provides a briefing on power structures as "hidden matters" that need to be addressed in order to achieve higher levels of business performance. A brief review of sources of power is provided, followed by a description of how organizational power has an effect on decision effectiveness.

Business improvement efforts are often thwarted because of hidden matters. It's the things that are hidden and undiscussed that end up causing us problems and difficulties. Decision effectiveness helps make the implicit explicit, and it takes what's normally hidden and brings it into the light for intelligent conversation and debate. The work of identifying key decisions and achieving clarity promotes productive conflict in leadership teams. In this respect, the discipline of decision effectiveness is a tool to navigate, interpret, and design the organizational power structures in a company.

Organizational Power

Power is a basic relational exchange that is deeply embedded in our human psyche and part of our personalities, characteristics, and tendencies (Singh, 2009). Organizational power in the right place, wielded in the right way, can generate enormous success. The flip-side is also true. Organizational power in the wrong place, wielded in the wrong way, can generate profound failure.

Human interactions with power and influence are as old as humanity itself. But, what is *power* exactly? One of the simplest

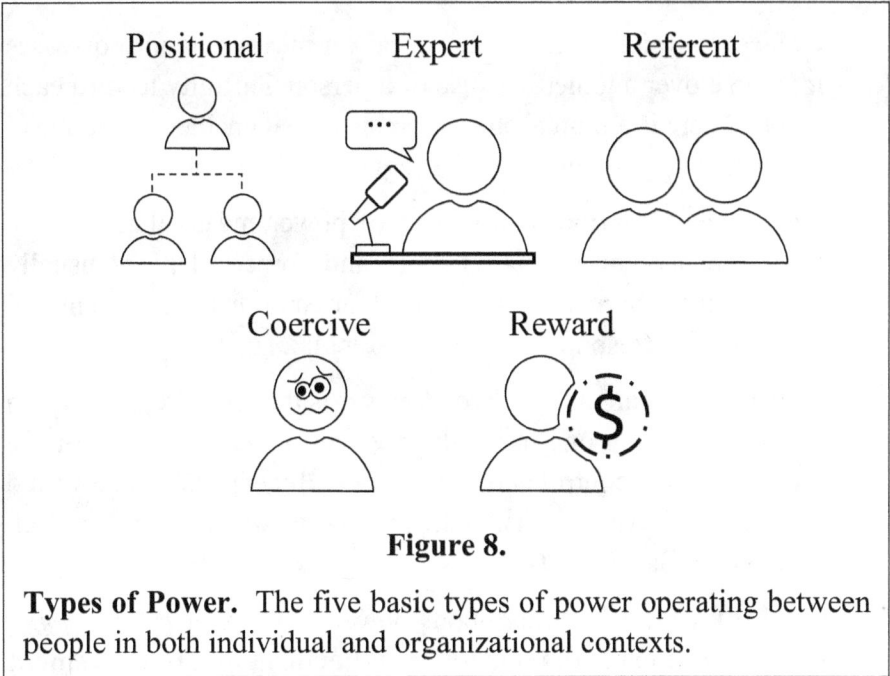

Figure 8.

Types of Power. The five basic types of power operating between people in both individual and organizational contexts.

expressions is that power is 'my ability to get you to do something that you wouldn't otherwise do.' Or, maybe it's something that you would do, but you wouldn't do it in the *way* I wanted, the *time* I wanted, or other variables that can be placed on the action. In other words, power is one's *influence* over another person. More formally, power is said to come in five sources or types as shown in Figure 8:

Positional: Position as a source of power means that one's ability to influence another comes from the role and position that is occupied. Quite literally, where you each are on the organizational chart.

Expert: Expertise as a source of power means that one possesses knowledge that the other does not; therefore, the one with the knowledge is in a place of influence because they are more competent.

Referent: Referent as a source of power means that one possesses influence over another because of a personal affinity toward each other. There is a mutual 'like' or respect that enables one to make a request and anticipate that the request will be honored.

Coercive: Coercion as a source of power means that one can influence another through threats and force. This is usually through either harm (physical, social, or emotional) or the removal of something (resources or relationships).

Reward: Reward as a source of power is the opposite of coercion and it means that one has influence with another because of the incentives they control and can provide. Incentives can be varied including physical, financial, assets, emotional, and social. (Sashkin & Sashkin, 2003).

Much of what is written about power deals with *interpersonal* power. In the context of **driving business performance improvement** and leveraging a **discipline** such as **decision effectiveness**, we are exclusively interested in power within an *organizational* context. Because of the organizational focus, we are interested in the assignment, use, retention, and transfer of power in a way that facilitates the optimum operation of the business.

To use organizational power in a way that benefits and optimizes the business, leaders will regularly need to move power away from *individual people* and ensure that power is placed with *roles* that are designed into the fabric of the business operation. When power structures are intentionally designed and alignment of decisional power is done *with roles*, the source of power is primarily **positional** and secondarily **expert**. When we intentionally align decision making authority and autonomy in this way we are saying that the decision belongs here because:

- This role is in the best place to make the call for the business

- Anyone who occupies this role will have the information they need
- They will see the data that supports the decision and best understand its implications on performance
- Any lower in the organization and the picture will be incomplete
- Any higher in the organization and the role will be too far removed from relevant detail, context, and information

The assignment of authority and autonomy through the design of roles makes a lot of sense. As a matter of fact, when businesses undertake organizational restructuring initiatives, it is this kind of design work that's being done. Though the decision-set is not explicitly dealt with in organizational design, the body of decisions is addressed through role descriptions and business unit segmentation. This is by no means a "hidden matter." To the contrary, this is explicit and usually formally communicated to the employee population. So, why then is organizational power a "hidden matter"? It is a hidden matter because it is the _hidden power structures_ that derail the formally designed and desired organizational structures and lines of authority. The decision effectiveness discipline can help to bring these power structures to the surface and subject them to intentional discussion, debate, and productive conflict that results in an optimized authority distribution.

Example:

Resetting Business Units and Centers of Excellence

Background: This company was number 2 in the entertainment industry. They had previously undergone several margin improvement initiatives through organizational restructuring. They had gone through a couple centralization and decentralization swings prompted by an equal number of financial leaders each of whom had their own values and opinions on the matter. The latest changes set up a strong culture of control by Finance and Accounting. Finance and Accounting operated the business by firmly rooting themselves as the control point for all procurement activities. Consequently, when project teams were in the Field working on customer accounts, all purchasing activities needed by the team had to go through Finance & Accounting. Operations literally could not purchase a pad of paper without approval.

This prompted two changes to business operations. First, the operations teams established an extensive planning process for all customer shows. This was done to get the most comprehensive build-lists in advance of a show, that way, in theory, all approvals could be rendered in advance. The consequence of this was a drastically increased cycle time for all customer shows. Second, the business hired an army of buyers who were assigned to customer field teams but reported directly to Finance and Accounting.

The reality of the entertainment business is that changes happen all the time in the Field. Customers change their mind. What looked good in concept drawings and on a plan document doesn't always look so good in real life; subsequently, there are field changes which have procurement needs. And, even though this "army of buyers" were with the field operations teams, their approval authorities were limited. Over 50% of their buys required corporate approval. This had the net-effect of slowing the show operations even further.

The Finance people were too far removed from the day-to-day operations, so while they made decisions that were based on economies of scale, the same decisions compromised customer service in the field. Over time this caused customers to find their own work-arounds, and procure their own designs, materials, and fixtures. So, while the margins did improve around what was sold, there was a backlash and overall revenue loss. Net effect was margin improvement on a rapidly reducing revenue stream.

Initiative: We were brought in under the premise that the company needed to conduct an organizational redesign. They had made changes in leadership within the operations groups, and the new leaders were of the opinion that there needed to be additional organizational changes in order to drive business financial improvements. They were correct; there needed to be some organizational restructuring. There was also a need for the company to address decision roles around key decisions that were impacting performance. And, to address these, there would also be impacts to processes and systems. At a minimum, the initiative required Organizational Design, Decision Effectiveness, Process Design, and Systems.

The effort started with an explicit strategy assessment of products, services, and market differentiation. We then reviewed critical organizational capabilities and where these needed to be placed in relationship to the customer. This led to a productive debate on the "role of the center" as we embarked upon the definitions of business units versus centers of excellence.

Legacy processes and systems left all buying and inventory decisions with Finance/Accounting. For better market performance, customer service, and improved market share, these buying decisions needed to be moved into Operations along with reasonable authority and accountability levels. It required redefining tables of authority in their ERP and Financial systems. It also required reworking procurement processes, forms, and review methods.

Outcome: First, were the organizational changes. The business units and COE's were formalized. Second, key decisions, roles, and rights were re-mapped to support the business objectives. This was done in parallel with the organizational changes being implemented. This way, when people landed in their new roles, they had clear authority and accountability for key decisions. Third, the systems and process changes were implemented. These took longer to implement, at around 90 days globally, so there was some discomfort in the new roles for a few months. This discomfort was managed exceptionally well though because everyone knew what decisions, authorities, and accountabilities were changing and *why* they were changing.

The business results were as-expected. The company was able to put in place the new organizational model, adjust key decision rights, modify process flows, and modify authority and workflows within their respective systems.

Results: The ecosystem approach and bundling of the 7 disciplines enabled the company to quickly improve the customer experience. The revenue trend flattened in 30 days and turned around toward growth in 60 days. A couple points of margin improvement were gained within 90 days because of the shifting of duties from Finance to the Field. Continued margin improvements were made at a slower pace because of the dependencies on a long-term business systems strategy.

Caveat: Yes, there is a caveat to taking this approach versus one discipline initiatives. While the issue that was presented to us was organizational structure, the cause of the performance gap required 3 other performance disciplines. As a matter of fact, had we only done the organizational piece, performance would not have changed. Because of the need to use 4 of the 7 performance disciplines (organization, decisioning, processes, and systems,) it took longer compared to other initiatives the company had implemented. *The old adage of "go slower to go faster" applies strongly.* Extra time spent to do it right yields tremendous long-term benefits. And, extra time doesn't mean what you might think. In this case it meant another 8-10 weeks in total consulting engagement time. (Internal work with IT continued for another three months after the engagement ended.) The biggest difference was that we had several workstreams active simultaneously so that the changes all interacted with each other when they needed to.

From Unwritten to Written Power Structures

The hidden matter of organizational *power* is contrasted with the written matter of organizational *structures, processes, and systems.* Written power structures are found in places such as organizational charts, process designs, and information technology and business systems. Indeed, processes and systems are two of the other six performance disciplines. They each address authority explicitly and in written form. Decision effectiveness is the only one of the seven disciplines that addresses the <u>unwritten</u> power structures. It is through the exercise of this discipline that leadership teams are able to change the unwritten to written.

Using the terms presented a few pages earlier in Figure 8, written structures correspond most to positional, coercive, and reward power. Unwritten structures correspond most to expert and referent power. If you have ever been part of an organization where it wasn't obvious how you need to acquire information and you had to learn who to go to for key information, you were experiencing unwritten expert power. The individual's role in providing information and guidance is undocumented, but everyone else seems to know who you should talk to. If you have ever been part of an organization where it wasn't obvious who you needed to "win over" before following the chain of command, you were experiencing unwritten referent power.

In the discipline of decision effectiveness, the unwritten expert and referent structures are explicitly discussed, analyzed, and defined. After decisions are written clearly, all roles are identified. The people who must provide input are recognized and differentiated by the type of input that's needed. Needing to agree with a recommendation before it comes forward to the decision-maker is part of the implementation of decision effectiveness. This identification and definition process itself promotes a high degree of productive conflict and debate, all the while keeping the focus on doing what's right for the business.

Summary

This was a short chapter, but a very important point of consideration. The ability for the discipline of decision effectiveness to deal with unwritten power structures is exceptionally useful. No other discipline can make the implicit explicit like this one can. No other discipline promotes the intellectual capital of a leadership team like this one. No other discipline fosters the level of productive conflict and resolution that this one does. It is a shame that so few have exposure to the discipline of decision effectiveness. To the extent that you and your leadership team commit yourselves to it, you can reap untold rewards and improvements for your business.

6. Thriving Together

Chapter Focus

To achieve improved business performance, it is necessary to take a systems approach with our companies. This chapter addresses two commonly used disciplines, decision effectiveness and organizational structure, and why they are insufficient to drive performance improvement on their own. The chapter closes with a brief treatment of the power of systems thinking and how the seven performance disciplines need to be bundled.

From the earlier chapter on "A Persistent Business Problem," it's clear that a new and revised approach is long overdue. Having a composite failure rate of 66% across our business initiatives is untenable and should not be tolerated by any leadership team. What if you could invert these statistics? What if you could achieve 90%+ _success_ rates? To achieve these levels it requires systems thinking specifically around all 7 performance disciplines.

Decision effectiveness cannot achieve high success levels by itself. It needs to be bundled with the right mix of the other disciplines in order to have an accretive effect. As previously explained though, decision effectiveness does boast a moderate positive correlation to performance improvement. When combined together, decision effectiveness is an excellent complement to all of the other six disciplines. Combining disciplines allows you to benefit from the accretive effect of positive correlations, and you can expect to have higher success rates than what is normally experienced through typical solo initiatives (where only one discipline is used.)

Insufficiency of Organization Structure by Itself

It is natural for a leader to take on a new role and in short-order call into question the organizational structure. Part of a new leadership role is the expectation of performance improvement. As a leader learns about their new business (or part of a business) they go through a set of questions about how that unit functions and where there might be opportunities for improvement. Organizational structure is one area that is quickly evident and in many cases glaringly obvious for improvements.

When it comes to organizational structure though, there is a big caution that needs to be stated and heard. If business performance improvement is what's desired, organizational structure changes should rarely (if ever) be undertaken *by themselves*. When done by itself, organizational structure has one of the lowest correlations to improving business performance. When measured in terms of profitability, organizational structure changes are only slightly correlated to performance improvement, one study showing a correlation of $0.17 - 0.19$ (Andersen & Jonsson, 2006). Another study showed a correlation at a "wee bit" stronger correlation of 0.285 (Mahalawat & Sharma, 2018). Given the previously mentioned failure statistics of organizational structure changes (72%), the slight correlation to performance makes sense.

If you've been in business leadership roles for a little while, your intuitively know that organization structure by itself is not strong enough to affect desirable performance changes. The reality is that most organizational design initiatives are never a pure structural design activity anyway. As much as practitioners strive to get business leaders to design organizational structures to truly fit the business, absent other considerations, it is not practical to do so. One of the most common concessions is with people. The fact is that we can only execute an organizational change which can be supported from a people-standpoint. We have the people we have for the most part. We can absorb, and may even desire, a percentage of change with people (e.g. 5%, 10%, maybe even 20%), but substantial and wholesale changes in people are simply impractical. Consequently, organizational structures are adjusted to fit the people situation. This is an example of bundling the organizational design discipline with the people discipline to drive improved execution. The biggest problem with only bundling *these two* together is that it increases the ability to execute the organizational changes, but it does not explicitly address the ability of the business to achieve the performance improvements that are needed. To do that we still need to invoke some of the other performance disciplines.

Insufficiency of Process by Itself

Process design is another common discipline for leaders to invoke when approaching business performance improvement. While processes boast a stronger correlation to economic benefit than organizational structure, they are still insufficient on their own. In one study, process improvements correlated at 0.42 to financial performance (Mahalawat & Sharma, 2018). As correlation coefficients go, 0.42 is a moderate correlation, colloquially, "pretty darned good." Similar results have been obtained in other recent studies (Sujova, Marcinekova, & Simanova, 2019).

Unfortunately, there is a phenomena that happens with the process discipline which is more pronounced than with the others. Process experts believe that *process* is the 1 solution to solve all our problems, but there is no such thing as the proverbial "silver bullet"/1-thing that will solve all our problems. Process design practitioners believe in the power of process design and management. Article after article proport the benefits of process design and maturity. The fact still remains that the correlation of process to business performance is moderate at-best.

Look, if any discipline were to ever achieve a correlation coefficient of 1.0, it would mean that 100% of the time invoking that discipline would directly result in improved business performance. There would be no need to do anything else. When you stop and think about any single effort having a correlation of 1.0 (100% positive result,) it is easy to quickly discern that such a correlation is both impossible and ridiculous. Yet, 1-discipline experts go around touting their single discipline as the answer to all your business problems. Stop believing them; it's tantamount to the modern-day version of the snake-oil-salesperson.

Let's be *real* about processes. Process design and management does boast one of the highest correlations to business performance improvement. As previously mentioned, processes have a moderate positive correlation. That's great; that means processes are useful! They still need to be bundled together in the right mix with the other disciplines to have the desired performance improvement on the business.

Insufficiency of Systems by Itself

When we see the word "systems" most of us will think of Information Technology (IT) systems. So, let's start there. Research studies that examine the relationship between investment in IT systems and improved financial performance of companies provide mixed feedback. Some show slightly positive correlations, while others show slight and moderate negative correlations (Fadhilah & Subriadi 2019; Kim, 2017; Sheng & Mykytyn, 2002; Shin, 2001). The resources listed here are but a sampling of what's available. As we have read and scanned the large number of studies, our general impression leaves us in the same place...it's a mixed review. Some positive and some negative.

There is one very strong theme that emerges from the research though: when IT systems investments are coupled with other interventions and disciplines, the correlation to company performance is positive. One particular study did a really nice job examining IT integration within supply chain (Kim, 2017). The study showed that IT investment by itself demonstrated a 0.15 correlation, which is not enough to claim as statistically significant; therefore, it confirms that IT investment by itself does not generate performance improvement. In the same study they examined coupling IT with supply chain integration efforts. The supply chain integration efforts included _process_ improvements for workflow both within the firm and with the firm's suppliers. (Notice the mixing of the _systems_ and _process_ disciplines here.) The supply chain integration process improvement efforts by themselves were able to demonstrate a 0.43 correlation to performance improvement, which again confirms the positive correlations in the prior section. Most notably, when the process work was combined with the IT systems work, the IT systems correlation jumped to 0.37. The company now benefits from the accretive effect of bundling the _systems_ and _process_ disciplines to generate better performance improvement.

When we examine systems, information systems are the only kind available to us. In today's world, information systems are ubiquitous, so it makes sense that we go there first. The systems landscape is vast. Here are a few types of systems: mechanical, biological, governmental, legal, communication, transport, and ergonomic. The list goes on and on, and in many cases different types of systems are combined to increase their efficacy. As a matter of fact, the fastest modes of innovation are the combining of IT systems with any and all other types of systems. From a company performance standpoint, the entire point of the systems discipline is that it helps ensure that work is performed in a predefined manner and with a high degree of accountability. With systems we are in-effect systematizing the work. When we do that we inextricably link the systems and process disciplines. This further underscores that fact that systems alone are insufficient to drive performance improvement; they must be bundled with one or more of the other disciplines.

Insufficiency of Tools by Itself

Admittedly, the discipline of Tools is not one that leaders think about all that often. When we bring it up in consulting engagements we often get blank looks and quiet rooms. It requires a bit of explanation to give it proper meaning and substance. Let's start with a definition. A tool is something that a person *needs* to complete a job; it is an *item* that's used which is *required* to *perform tasks*. Let's look at two examples.

We had an industrial manufacturing client where we were doing some follow-up work on their employee survey. Engagement levels had dropped at one of their plants, and we were also seeing dissatisfaction with both processes and tools. We conducted some focus groups on site to go a little deeper and determine the root cause(s) of the issues. In the last focus group of the day, we found it. When we asked the question, "What's frustrating about working here?" one of the line workers in the Final Assembly Department spoke up. She said that a couple months ago management had taken away their good air-impact-wrenches and instead given them poor quality replacements. She further related that their entire department relied on these wrenches all day and every day. She understood why they did this; they were trying to consolidate the different types of air wrenches they bought and gain some leverage out of buying in bulk. The problem was that all the other departments used their air wrenches periodically; they were not integral tools to every job. Someone else from the same department spoke up, and he said that they further restricted replacements. They would only receive replacements monthly. Because of the usage volume, the current air wrenches would break somewhere in the second or third week. Then, for the last one or two weeks of the month, their production volume and quality would drop. The department was getting in trouble for this drop in volume, but it wasn't their fault. They said it was caused by this subpar air wrench. After the focus group, we walked the plant floor and then inquired with the management. It was confirmed; there was a tool issue that was having a dramatic impact on throughput. Once fixed, volume and quality were restored, which had a direct impact on fulfillment and revenue.

We had a client that was reworking its sales and customer-deal-review process. As a large business-to-business company, historically executing large contracts on a global basis, the deal review process had historically been something that was conducted at a global-region level. Over the years though, the customer base had become more and more occupied by smaller and smaller companies. Consequently, the deals being executed had also gotten smaller and smaller over time. They wanted to push the decision making down into the organization so the process could be executed more quickly. They approached the change by using the *process* and *decision* disciplines, and they redesigned the deal review to occur at a lower level. Several months later the company noticed that the quality of the deals that were being approved had suffered, and this was causing a higher rate of charge-offs (inability to collect.) When we re-engaged with the company, what we discovered was a tools issue. The processes and decisioning was working properly, but there was a low level of consistency around the evaluation of a deal. In partnership, we developed a deal-review template, which was subsequently implemented around the world. This template functioned as a common *tool* and ensured that all teams were examining a minimum set of criteria. Several months later the company also implemented the tool through and IT system. In this case they ended up bundling together processes, decisioning, tools, and systems to gain the performance improvements needed.

We are awash with tools nowadays. Many times, businesses that are tool-sensitive are aware of that sensitivity. Industry segments like manufacturing, medical care, and automotive repair are a few good examples of businesses that are tool sensitive. At the same time, _all businesses_ have a set of tools that are needed to execute their value chain. You may be in a business where your toolset and IT systems are one in the same; this is often true for businesses that are comprised of information and knowledge workers. Most of us will land somewhere in between these two extremes, so it's is useful to ask the question. When the tools discipline needs attention, its impact on performance is huge.

There are some useful case studies and research such as Coulson-Thomas, 2005 and Henning, 2010. However, we have found no recent empirical research studies which would provide statistical correlations for this discipline. You would have to go back to the first half of the 20th century, during the height of the industrial age, to read empirical research studies about job tools. In today's age, we will instead speak from experience. From our experience working with clients in real-world applications, we would place the correlation as moderate…about on-pace with processes. The biggest difference we've seen is that the impact on performance is usually indirect and removed by two degrees or more; it requires effort to research and analyze the root cause of the performance gap and trace it back to job tools. If the gap is discovered to be caused by missing or improperly specified tools, correcting the issue has immediate and observable impacts on downstream performance. Tools is an equally critical performance discipline and should not be overlooked.

Insufficiency of People by Itself

In the past 10 years, the People discipline has received a substantial increase in attention, and a significant body of empirical evidence is being built which demonstrates its correlation to performance. The People discipline includes the body of work that is most closely related to strategic human resources and organizational development/effectiveness. This includes work such as talent, culture, leadership, and learning.

The correlations reported in the body of research positions the People discipline as having a 0.31 correlation to company performance (Loshali & Krishnan, 2013). The same study reviewed the impact of transformational leadership in firm performance and found that it had a correlation of 0.33. If you go back 10-15 years ago, there was a substantial *lack* of empirical research; opinions about the impact of people-activities on performance were mixed (Wright, et al, 2005). Today's body of research supports a slightly positive correlation of the People discipline to company performance.

As the heading suggests, this discipline is not enough by itself. Like the other disciplines, practitioners in the people discipline are prone to promote their discipline as the "silver bullet" of performance improvement. The more prevalent of these seems to be those practitioners who focus on leadership. We don't want to give you the wrong impression here; leadership is important! Strong transformational leadership has a positive correlation of 0.33 (Loshali & Krishnan, 2013). Other empirical studies place it higher and some place it a bit lower, so we picked a middle point. But, don't get lulled into thinking that having the absolute best leader with the absolute best inspirational messaging is the only secret to your success; it is not. It is *one of many pieces* to the puzzle that once completed will generate the business performance desired.

A really good analogy here is with sports teams. Our favorite sport in our home is U.S. football, and with a little bit of research you can probably figure out which team we follow. In football (like all other sports,) if a team spends a bunch of money on talent, it does not guarantee that they will out-perform every other team. Even with the best talent that money can buy, the team still requires all of the other disciplines to deliver optimal performance. It needs the right organizational structure, from ownership all the way down through the ball club. Decision effectiveness and decision rights need to be mapped and understood by everyone, especially on the field of play. It's disastrous to try to play ball when no one knows who's recommending plays and who has the final decision. All surrounding processes need to work seamlessly. The field-of-play processes are practiced day-in and day-out until they become second nature. Systems surround the team from operations, information; the most notable to fans are the statistical systems that are ever-present. Incentives are significant and help drive performance too. In the middle of all this is the *People* discipline with the right talent, development, leadership, and culture. When it all comes together, you have the thrill of competing at the big game.

The research body shows us that the People discipline has a slight positive correlation to performance. By itself it is insufficient to achieve high levels of success. Bundled together correctly with the other performance disciplines, the effects are accretive and substantial. That is the essence of the seven performance disciplines; they are powerful when mixed properly.

Insufficiency of Incentives by Itself

Incentives is the final performance discipline that we'll address in this section. It also is insufficient by itself to drive substantial performance improvement. We have been asked through the years why we separated incentives from the people discipline. The question is expected. If incentives were only a point of consideration for employees, subordinating it to the People discipline would make sense. However, incentives play a large role throughout a company's ecosystem. As companies, we are regularly reviewing how we incentivize both upstream and downstream in our supply chains. Remuneration and pay conditions get buried inside contracts, service level agreements, and pricing schedules; none-the-less, they are vitally important to a company's performance. The ability to address incentives both internally and externally to a company is the reason for naming this a separate discipline.

The body of research around the correlation of incentives to performance is broad and deep. There are a large number of studies to select from. When examining internal/employee incentives, one of the more consistent positive correlations of incentives to performance is in the area of sales. Studies will report this correlation typically from 0.3 to 0.4; this study by Nourayi and Krishnan report the correlation at 0.407 (2006). Like the other disciplines, this places incentives in the territory of being slightly positive to performance. When examining correlations to other measures of performance such as shareholder return and return on assets, the numbers drop dramatically to less than 0.1 and end up being statistically insignificant (albeit still positive.) Other studies report similar correlations and relationships (Aggarwal & Samwick, 2006; Bushman, et al, 2016) In companies where innovation is key, studies have supported positive correlations between incentives and innovation; however, large pay differential among employees actually inverts the correlation and creates a disincentive (Yanadori & Cui, 2013).

Supply chain performance and incentives have a story to tell too. Incentives which address inventory and delivery performance have show to be particularly effective (Cohen, et al, 2007). Monitoring systems that provide clear performance indicators against agreed service levels work best. One of the best research studies we've found on supplier studies examined both cooperative and competitive incentives (Regis & Krause, 2015). Both cooperative and competitive incentives had a slightly positive correlation to performance in each measured category: delivery, quality, and cost. The correlations ranged from 0.06 to .022.

Again, like the other disciplines, incentives have a slightly positive correlation to performance. It would seem that the strongest correlation is in the area of sales performance. However, in most areas we've researched the relationships are shown to be positive. The one to note is when incentives have a large differential/dispersion among employees. Some of the research shows that allowing this to happen creates a negative correlation and disincentivizes performance.

Summary

One truth about the 7 performance disciplines, each of them can be over-used. When over-used, they detract from performance. Like all the other disciplines, too much process is a bad thing. Over-applied, processes have a negative impact on organizational performance (Gleeson, 2016; Bodell, 2012). Too much process can be bad. Processes were made for people; people were not made for processes. Processes should serve, enable, and improve the business. If they do not, then they need to be redesigned. And, that redesign may very well be a process simplification to *remove* bureaucracy and streamline workflow.

What needs to be realized is that organizational structure and processes are two change levers that are *interdependent* with the other 5 change levers. The organizational structure defines and *implies* roles, responsibilities, authority levels, and workflow. The organizational chart is a method of communication, to the company, about each of these. If changes are made on an **organizational** chart, but **decision/authority rights** are not defined and communicated, the company will end up with people in roles who cannot effectively execute the duties of their jobs as intended. If work **processes** aren't changed to match, the people in the new structure are left guessing about what changes in work activities management really wanted from them…who knows what kind of workflow changes will be gained, if any. If **systems** requirements and changes aren't defined to match the new organizational structure, any automated workflow, approvals, and movement of information won't occur; thereby, it would have the effect of crippling the intended authority levels and decision effectiveness of the roles. Avoid the consideration of **tools**, and people will not be able to fulfill what was a well-intended design (e.g. If a new leadership role is not enabled with the right reports and analytics, the decision quality will suffer.) Put in place a great organizational structure and put **people** in roles that aren't a good fit for them, and performance will often drop precipitously along with the unintended development of negative team dynamics. Some would go so far as to say, 'if you put in place the right **incentives**, the rest of it will fall in place.' Without a doubt, the right incentive design is crucial for motivating both work activities and performance outcomes, but incentives work in conjunction with organizational structure and the other disciplines. Changes in any one of the 7 disciplines carry subsequent changes in the others: **organizational structure, decision rights**, **processes, systems, tools, people**, and **incentives**. Successful performance improvement requires a multidisciplinary approach.

7. Decision Models & Methods

<table>
<tr><td>

Chapter Focus

This chapter briefly reviews foundational models in decisioning such as rational and intuitive decisioning. It further explores the rational methods of making decisions and illustrates how those methods can be selected to help ensure decision criterion are met: quality, speed, effort.

</td></tr>
</table>

Decision effectiveness, like many other things in life, has been studied for a long time. There are many other earlier works, studies, and reports that can be referenced. The acronyms that have been reviewed so far assume a *group* process for decision making. But, there are other approaches to decision making. We will start with an overview of the rational and intuitive models. Then, we will review each of rational methods, and we'll end with group decision making. This will give us a springboard to go deeper with group decision making and build on the content already presented. We will fully examine the anatomy of a decision, in a way that enables companies and teams of people to collaboratively participate in *effective* decision making.

Rational and Intuitive Models

As human beings we conduct two fundamental types of decision making, rational and intuitive. Rational decision making is like it sounds, where we apply intentional thought, weigh alternatives, and arrive at an analyzed and informed choice. Intuitive decision making is like it sounds, where we arrive at a choice through intuition or a "gut reaction." As we learned in an earlier chapter, psychology refers to these two types of decision processes in a parallel *thinking* framework called System 1 and System 2 thinking. System 1 thinking is the intuitive and System 2 thinking is rational. If you are a quality oriented individual it may be tempting to believe that rational decision-making is better than intuitive decision-making. It is generally true that rational decisions have a higher quality outcome than intuitive ones. However, rational thinking requires more effort, resources, and energy to conduct; therefore, it is also slower.

If you're walking down a nature trail and are suddenly charged by a brown bear that's 8-10 times your weight and running toward you at 20mph/32kph, it is unlikely that a slow and rational decisioning process is going to save your life. In this case, you'd better be able to render a fast and intuitive decision that yields your safety as an outcome. This is why the military has the saying, "train as you fight, fight as you train." In essence they're saying that you should apply rational thinking when you train, so that during training your efforts are intentional, planful, accurate, and result in the outcomes desired. Additionally, train it through repetition so it becomes second-nature and intuitive. This is also the cornerstone of all martial arts and linguistics. Tai Chi is a great example of the precept. Known for its fluid movements, it's often viewed as an art form that the young and old perform because it promotes balance, flexibility, and strength. However, it is less known that the movements performed in Tai Chi mirror the more aggressive combat forms. Actually, Tai Chi is not an art, it is considered a game and when one participates, it is said that you *play* Tai Chi. It mirrors the other two forms of Bagua Zhang and Xingyi, all three of which are part of the family of Chinese martial arts known as Wushu. "Train as you fight, and fight as you train." The parallel is true in our organizations when we are learning how to make decisions differently. We must use System 2 thinking to slow down and practice, with the goal to commit the new method to a more intuitive System 1 thinking process.

SIDRC

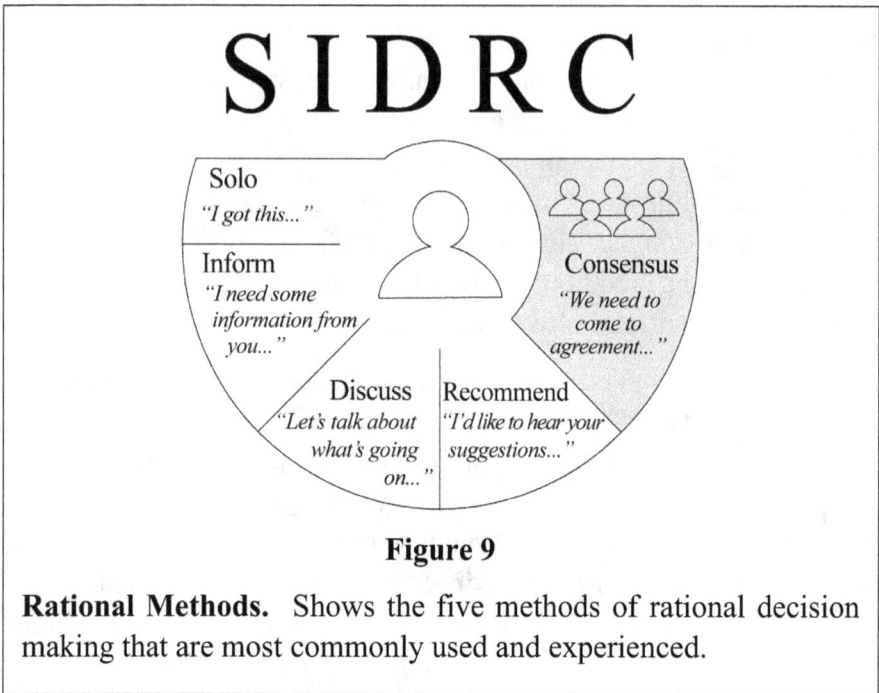

Solo
"I got this..."

Inform
"I need some information from you..."

Consensus
"We need to come to agreement..."

Discuss
"Let's talk about what's going on..."

Recommend
"I'd like to hear your suggestions..."

Figure 9

Rational Methods. Shows the five methods of rational decision making that are most commonly used and experienced.

Psychology Today reported that an average person makes 35,000 decisions per day (Guttman, 2019). That's a lot of decisions, and they range from the small to the large. Most of these decisions are made through System 1/intuitive thinking. Remember the last time you went through a routine and then a little while later you looked back on it and said, 'I don't remember what I just did.' You executed that routine using System1/intuitive thinking. Common occurrences are getting ready in the morning and the daily commute to work. These are things that we normally <u>do</u> think about and we normally <u>do</u> render some degree of System 2/rational thought, but when we need it, our System 1/intuitive thinking takes over and executes the routine seamlessly. Our System 1/intuitive thinking center of our brain is responsible for the bulk of those 35,000 decisions per day. Without it, we would quite literally be paralyzed and unable to function. The resource requirements of executing all 35,000 decisions through System

2/rational thinking is too high and our brains are not capable of meeting those requirements. We need System 1/intuitive thinking.

We also need System 2/rational thinking, but to fully optimize we have to apply rational thinking in situations where it is needed and most beneficial. Rational decision making involves following a logical order of steps that formally considers the situation/problem, weighs alternatives, and resolves a course of action. And, to be fair to the body of work around decision making, what most of us conduct in a business setting is what's called 'bounded rational decision making.' We are bound by constraints where we cannot consider every possible combination and permutation of a solution but rather we choose from a set of alternatives that is perceived as *best* in the *context* of current circumstances.

Within our business settings, there are different *methods* of bounded-rational decision making (Vroom & Yetton, 1973). These *methods* are shown in Figure 9. The labels have been simplified from the original work of Vroom and Yetton. The labeling is done from the perspective and participation of others, such as other team members or coworkers.

The first method of decision making is **Solo**. *Solo* decision making is where an individual acts exclusively from their own authority and autonomy. Like it says in the figure the approach is, "I got this." They individually assess a situation, review alternatives, and select the best course of action. This is all done without interacting with or requiring any kind of input from any other team members. In today's information-age, if you collect information online for the purposes of making a decision, and you do not interact with a person, you are performing the solo method of decision making.

The second method of decision making is **Inform**. *Inform* decision making is where an individual acts with information provided by others. The individual is still very much acting independently and exercising the highest degree of authority and autonomy. They assess the situation, review alternatives, and select the best course of action on their own. The difference between *inform* and *solo* is that in the *inform* case, the individual does not have all the information they need, nor can they get it on their own, so they must request it from other people. It takes the shape of, "I need some information from you." There is no dialogue other than an information request which takes place between the decider and those providing information.

The third method of decision making is **Discuss**. *Discuss* decision making is where an individual acts with information provided by others, but because of the nature of the *discussion*, the others provide contextually relevant and targeted information. The focus of this method in the work by Vroom and Yetton (1973) further restricted this by eliminating any group meetings; the discussion was between the decider and each individual separately, and it has an attitude summarized by, "Let's talk about what's going on." Such a distinction is not necessary for our purposes, and as a matter of fact, group discussion does prove useful in many cases. Our goal is to drive improved decision effectiveness, so in the application of the *discuss* method, we should not preclude group discussions. In this method people are providing information, analyses, opinions, and interpretations, but no one in the group goes so far as to make an actual recommendation; that is the next method.

The fourth method of decision making is **Recommend**. *Recommend* decision making is where an individual acts not only with information provided by others but also acts upon a *recommendation* that is provided by any or all of the team members. This is a group-rich consultative method where each member potentially contributes material information, has expertise with the situation, and can effectively contribute to reviewing alternatives and selecting among the best. The individual decider still retains a high degree of authority and autonomy to make the choice, but it is a heavily influenced choice where they in-effect are saying to the group, "I'd like to hear your suggestions." Of note: the *recommend* method is the focus of both the DECIDE and RAPIDS decision rights models. Also of note is that decision rights coding schema often only focus on the recommend method, and they exclude the other 4 methods of decision making.

The fifth method of decision making is **Consensus**. *Consensus* decision making changes the focal point of the decision and moves it away from an individual to a *group* of people who must, _as a group_, *concur* with the choice. When an individual occupies a central role in the *consensus* method it is to function as a *facilitator*. Others are involved in the process, providing information, conducting analyses, and generating alternatives and recommendations. Ultimately though it is the *group* of peers who each have equal authority and accountability for the decision and its outcome. They look around at each other and say, "We need to come to agreement." There are variations of consensus that can be applied. In the truest sense of the word, consensus means 'general agreement.' There are some who believe that consensus means 100% agreement or unanimity, but this is neither to the definition of the word nor to the reality of implementation. Variations of 'general agreement' can be applied though, tempering consensus with democratic-like voting where simple majority or super-majority can determine the group's choice. All forms of parliamentary procedure focus on the consensus method.

Which Decision-Method Should You Use?

The short answer to this question is: All of them! It's almost certain that you use all of them in your business today. Figure 10 shows a decision tree that Vroom and Yetton (1973) described in their book. While we use all of these methods for getting decisions made, we don't normally go through such an explicit and structured way to determine how to engage in decisioning. This decision tree presents a series of 7 questions that can be asked, and the answers to the questions leads you through the tree to select an appropriate method of decision making: Solo, Inform, Discuss, Recommend, or Consensus.

The model presupposes essentially two organizing themes: quality and people. The first question in the tree around quality is there to help derive the approach to decision-making in reference to people. All subsequent questions are oriented to achieving high quality or low quality while helping to figure out how to best engage people. It's a fairly intuitive tree to follow, and it makes a lot of sense upon first examination.

A gap in the model as presented by Vroom and Yetton (1973) is that it considers *only* the presence or absence of a *quality* dimension. As previously examined, the triple constraints theory tells us that there are 3 organizing dimensions: quality, speed, and cost. Consequently, a decision tree as presented by Vroom and Yetton completely ignores the fact that *speed* of decision making is sometimes more important than quality, or that a *low-cost* decision is more important than quality. As we read earlier, all of these dimensions are important when it comes to achieving higher levels of decision effectiveness. Role clarity, quality, speed, effort, and yield must all be optimized for maximum effectiveness.

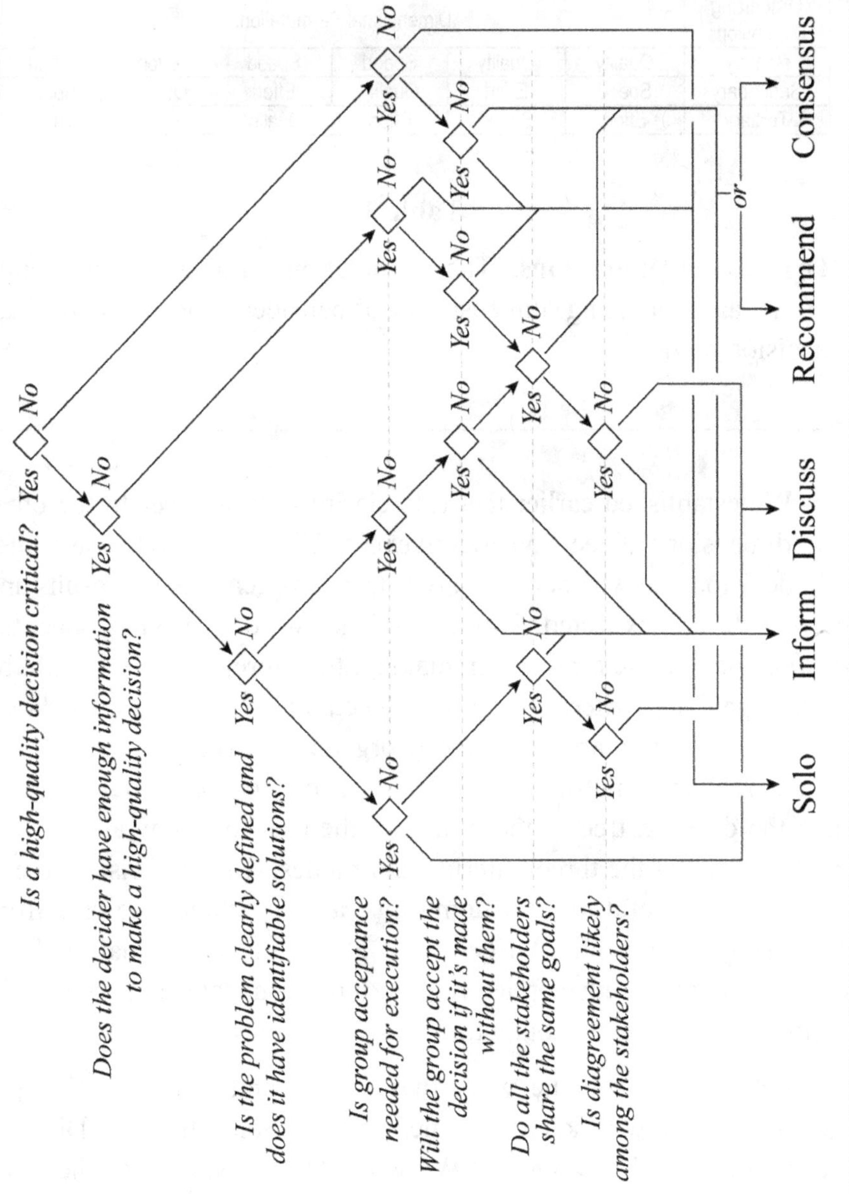

Figure 10

Decision Tree. An example of a decision tree to help determine which type of decision-making method might be appropriate.

Organizing Dimensions	Dimensional Permutations					
Primary	Quality	Quality	Speed	Speed	Effort	Effort
Secondary	Speed	Effort	Quality	Effort	Quality	Speed
Tertiary	Effort	Speed	Effort	Quality	Speed	Quality

Table 3

Organizing Dimensions. The permutations of quality, speed, and effort as organizing dimensions to consider when selecting a decision model.

We established earlier that role clarity is an *enabler* to the other four dimensions of decision effectiveness. Yield refers to the outcomes of a decision and whether or not our decisions generate the results and outputs that we expected. Neither of these two dimensions impact the *method* that we use for decision making; therefore, we are left with the three organizing criterion: Quality, Speed, and Effort. Table 3 shows the various permutations of these organizing criterion. To do an exhaustive job of putting together a decision tree, one would need to map the decision tree so that it allows the user to follow all possible permutations of the three criterion and modes. But, a decision tree is not the most useful tool for doing this, as it precludes the user from exercising judgement. All decisions are highly contextual, and the criterion and methods applied require intelligent selection which will yield the most effective output.

Let's expand on the work that Vroom and Yetton (1973) put forward. We will keep the methods of Solo, Inform, Discuss, Recommend, and Consensus. We will add alongside these the three criteria mentioned in the preceding paragraph: quality, speed, and effort. Table 4 illustrates what this decision-method-selection would look like when it's expanded. The left three columns define the decision criterion, and the right five columns indicate which method(s) are most likely to yield the criterion selected.

A major constraint you should be aware of when applying this table: the size of the company and number of employees matters. For example, a micro company with only a few employees would be more inclined to use *solo, inform,* and *discuss.* At the other end of the continuum, a conglomerate with a hundred thousand employees would be more inclined to use *discuss, recommend,* and *consensus.*

A second major constraint you should be aware of when applying this table: type of organization matters. For example, a democratic-like governing organization will be more inclined to use *recommend* and *consensus*; whereas an autocratic-like governing organization will be more inclined to use *solo, inform,* and *discuss.*

Criteria			Methods				
Quality	Speed	Effort	Solo	Inform	Discuss	Rcmd.	Consensus
H	H	H	○	◐	●	◐	○
H	H	M	○	◐	●	◐	○
H	H	L	○	◐	●	○	○
H	M	H	○	◐	●	●	●
H	M	M	○	◐	●	●	●
H	M	L	○	◐	●	○	○
H	L	H	○	◐	●	●	●
H	L	M	○	◐	●	●	●
H	L	L	○	◐	●	○	○
M	H	H	◐	◐	●	◐	○
M	H	M	●	●	●	◐	○
M	H	L	◐	●	◐	○	○
M	M	H	◐	◐	◐	●	●
M	M	M	◐	●	●	●	●
M	M	L	●	●	●	○	○
M	L	H	◐	◐	◐	●	●
M	L	M	◐	●	●	●	●
M	L	L	◐	●	●	○	○
L	H	H	◐	●	●	◐	○
L	H	M	●	●	●	◐	○
L	H	L	●	●	◐	○	○
L	M	H	◐	◐	●	●	●
L	M	M	◐	◐	●	●	●
L	M	L	●	●	◐	○	○
L	L	H	◐	◐	◐	●	●
L	L	M	◐	●	●	●	●
L	L	L	●	●	◐	○	○

Table 4

Decision Criteria and Methods. Table showing the most likely methods that will deliver the decision criteria needed, exploring all combinations of decision criteria on a low, medium, high scale.

Key		
Least Likelihood	**Medium Likelihood**	**Most Likelihood**
○	◐	●

Understanding the relationship between decision criterion and decision-making methods is important to selecting the right method and driving maximum decision effectiveness. First, some assumptions that will help you understand how Table 4 is populated and subsequently how it is used:

- **High Quality:** When high quality is the prevailing criteria, the method least likely to deliver is solo. The old adages apply: 'Two heads are better than one," or, "All of us together are better than any of us alone." If we need high quality, we are going to have to interact with each other in some manner. Therefore, solo is the least effective method.
- **High Speed:** When high speed (fast) is the prevailing criteria, the method least likely to deliver is consensus. Getting a group to consensus is the slowest of all methods, and the higher the level of consensus needed the slower the decision making (e.g. unanimous vs. super-majority vs. simple majority). Next in line is when a group is required to work together to generate formal recommendations; while not as slow as consensus, it is still, by its nature, significantly slower than solo, inform, or discuss.
- **Low Effort:** When low effort (low cost) is the prevailing criteria, the methods least likely to deliver are consensus and recommend. Both are relatively high cost methods requiring the use of more extensive people resources and carrying higher operational expenditure implications.

Using Table 4, let's go through six examples, which are highlighted in the table. These six are chosen because they are the most common. When we force ourselves to rank order the triple constraints and identify primary, secondary, and tertiary, these are six combinations that become prevalent:

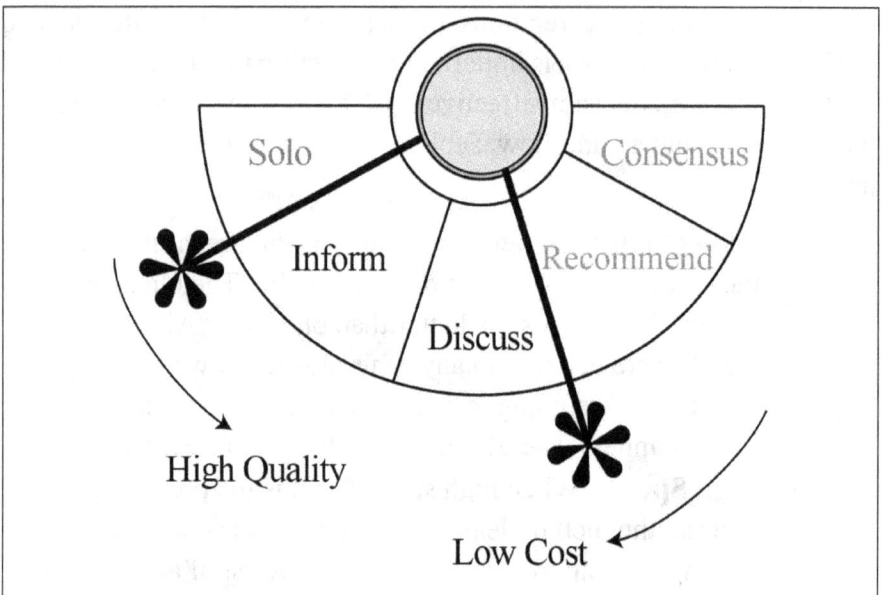

Figure 11

Decision Method Selection, H-M-L. Showing how method selection levers would move based on the need for high quality, medium speed, and low cost.

H – M – L | High Quality, Medium Speed, Low Cost:

Refer to Table 4 and Figure 11. The need for high quality pushes us to the right; whereas, the need for low cost pushes us to the left. Consequently, *solo, recommend,* and *consensus* are least likely to yield the outcome. From a quality standpoint, *informing* is better than *solo*, but because there is no dialogue about the context of the decision, this method receives a lower rating. From a cost standpoint, *recommend* is still costly to implement as a method because of the people and operational expenditures; therefore, it receives a least-likely rating. The best rated approach for this set of criterion is the *discuss* method, which allows for dialogue around the context of the problem/issue without requiring work to be done to generate formal recommendations. By using the *discuss* method we get the benefit of group interactions without the cost of producing formal recommendations.

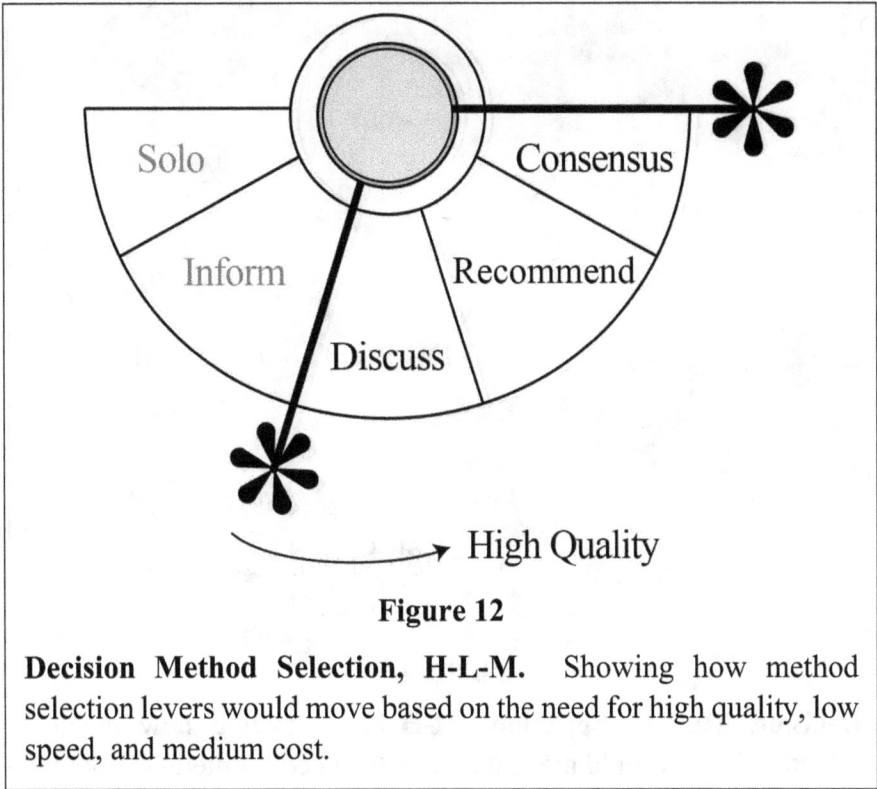

Figure 12

Decision Method Selection, H-L-M. Showing how method selection levers would move based on the need for high quality, low speed, and medium cost.

H – L – M | High Quality, Low Speed, Medium Cost:

Refer to Table 4 and Figure 12. The primary need for high quality pushes us to the right; whereas, the tolerance of slower speed opens methods on the right. All three of the methods on the right, *discuss*, *recommend*, and *consensus* are open for selection. The tolerance for slow speed would provide further impetus for using either *recommend* or *consensus*. Additional judgement on the context of the problem and issue and fuller cost/benefit understanding will be beneficial in selecting a method that will be most effective for the organization.

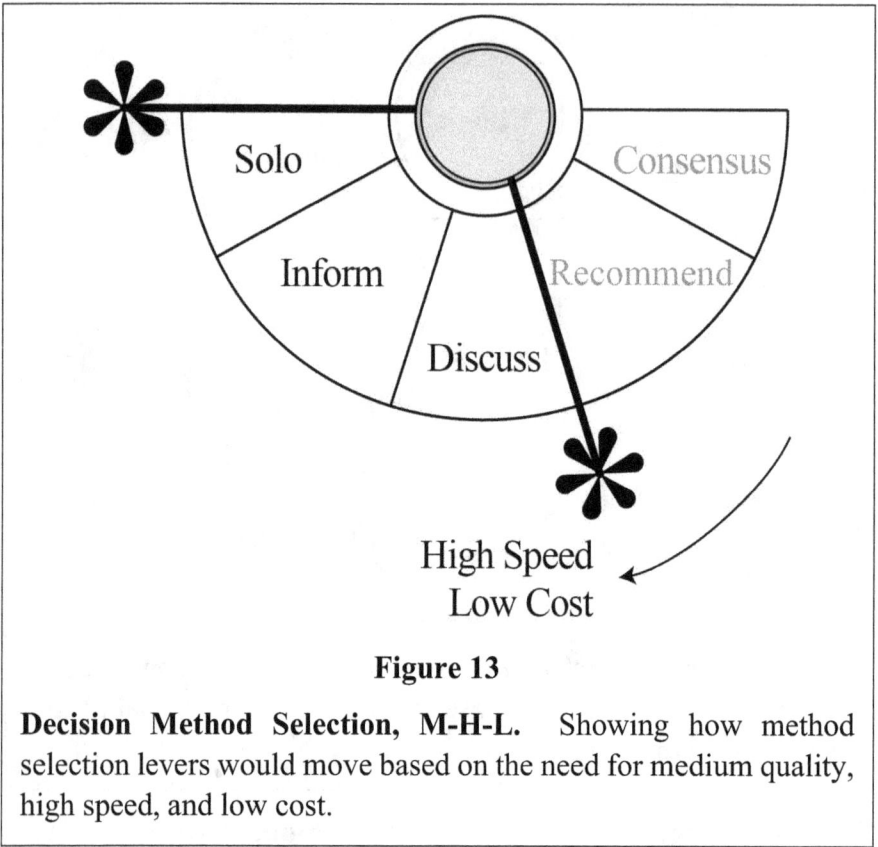

Figure 13

Decision Method Selection, M-H-L. Showing how method selection levers would move based on the need for medium quality, high speed, and low cost.

M – H – L | Medium Quality, High Speed, Low Cost:

Refer to Table 4 and Figure 13. The primary need for high speed pushes us to the left; subsequently, the secondary need for low cost also pushes us to the left. *Consensus* and *recommend* are both higher cost because of the people and operational expense. Group methods are also slower, so these become the least likely to yield the selected criterion. *Solo, inform,* and *discuss* are the three methods most likely to yield the selected criterion. The counter-balancing needs for both medium quality and low cost would tend to lead one to the *inform* method as optimal.

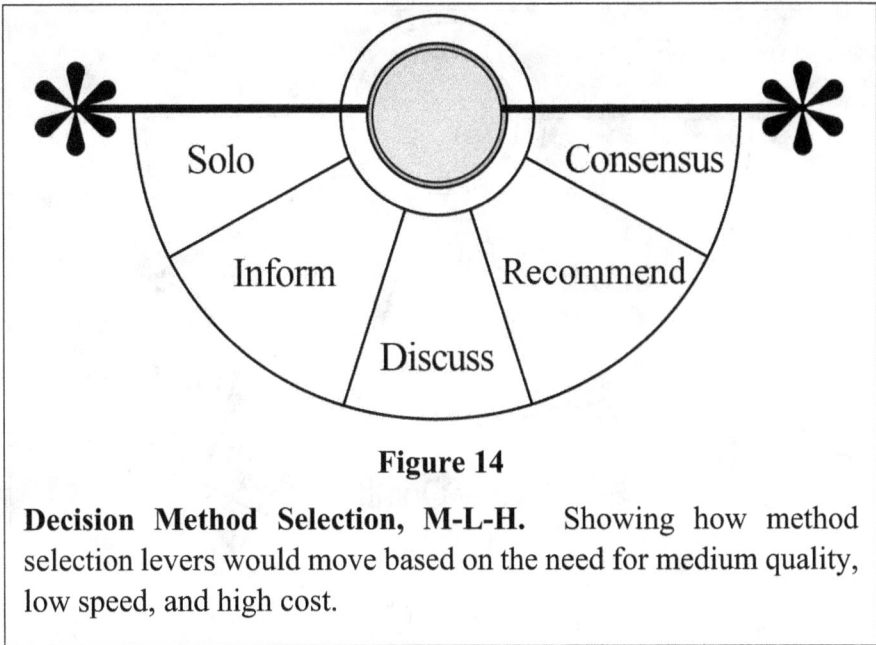

Figure 14

Decision Method Selection, M-L-H. Showing how method selection levers would move based on the need for medium quality, low speed, and high cost.

M – L – H | Medium Quality, Low Speed, High Cost:

Refer to Table 4 and Figure 14. While this is 1 of the 6 scenarios created by forced ranking, this set of criterion is probably not one that any of us are really going to have the luxury of working with. Effectively, these criterion are saying that we want to be slow, cost a lot, and will accept a moderate level of quality. If you happen to land on this set of criterion, you have a lot of options. The tolerance of slow speed and high cost opens the options on the right. The ability to tolerate medium quality also makes the left two options somewhat likely. Decision context will govern the choice of method, and if you end up considering this mix of criterion and methods, it is quite possible that it's because of the need for consensus; therefore, it flips the situation around and method drives criterion.

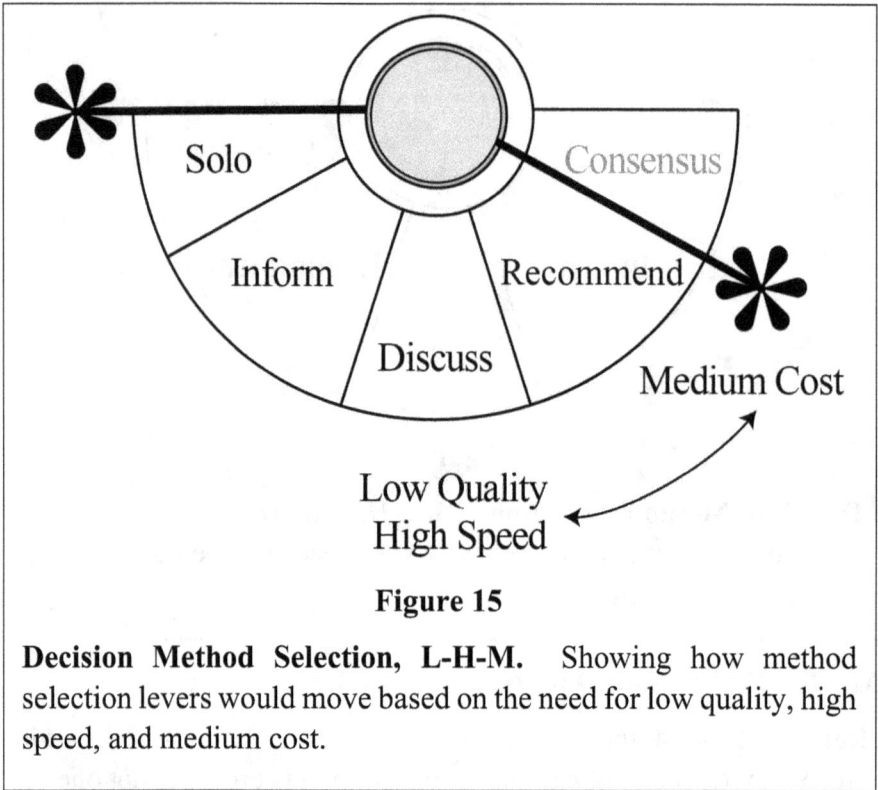

Figure 15

Decision Method Selection, L-H-M. Showing how method selection levers would move based on the need for low quality, high speed, and medium cost.

L – H – M | Low Quality, High Speed, Medium Cost:

Refer to Table 4 and Figure 15. The need for high speed and tolerance of low-quality pushes us to the left. By themselves, these two criterion would eliminate both *consensus* and *recommend*; however, the ability to tolerate a medium level of cost re-opens the possibility of using *recommend*. *Consensus* becomes the least likely to yield the selected criterion because of the primary need for speed. Even though the cost tolerance opens up the use of recommend, the most likely methods able to yield the criterion are *solo, inform, and discuss*.

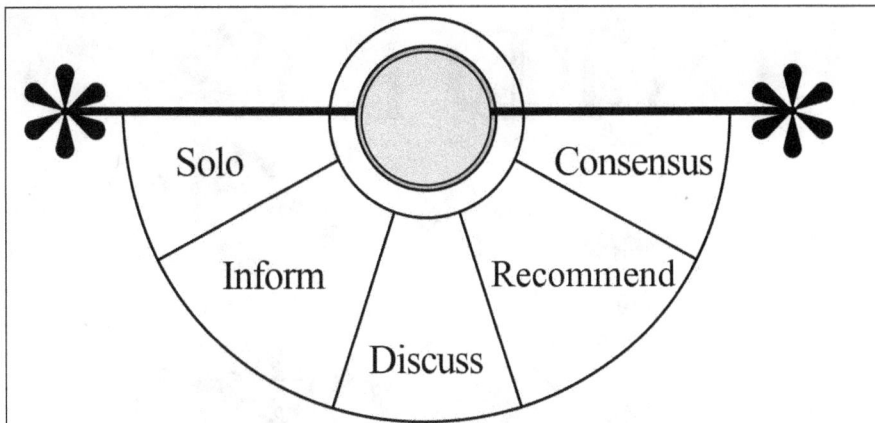

Figure 16

Decision Method Selection, L-M-H. Showing how method selection levers would move based on the need for low quality, medium speed, and high cost.

L – M – H | Low Quality, Medium Speed, High Cost:

Refer to Table 4 and Figure 16. Similar to the mix described a couple paragraphs earlier, this too could be a situation where the need for consensus drives the expected criterion. If you happen to land on this set of criterion, you have a lot of options. The tolerance of medium speed and high cost opens the options on the right. The ability to tolerate low quality also makes the left two options likely. Decision context will govern the choice of method.

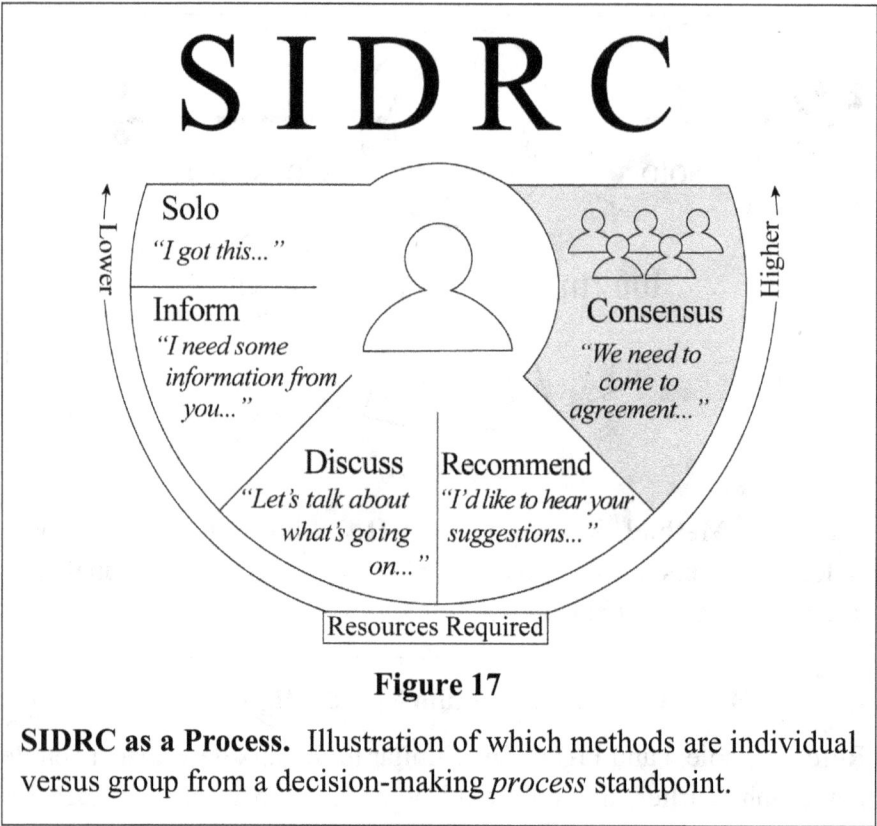

Figure 17

SIDRC as a Process. Illustration of which methods are individual versus group from a decision-making *process* standpoint.

Let's come back to the SIDRC model that was adapted from Vroom and Yetton (1973). We're going to modify the graphic that was presented in Figure 9 to better distinguish between the individual and the group. When initially proposed, Vroom and Yetton were focused on the decider – the entity that actually makes the decision. In this respect the previous figure is an accurate depiction of their initial proposal because it is decider focused. However, when we're running a business, we have a great use for understanding the decision-making process, because there's a lot more at work than just the decider. The further to right in this model, the more organizational resources are required to execute a decision process. As Figure 17 shows, *solo* and *inform* are individual-centric methods of decision making. Discuss and recommend are really hybrids, where they use a group-centric process but still retain a single decider. Whereas, consensus is a wholly group-centric method where the process and the decision are completed by the group.

When to Use the Consensus Method

Some would have you believe that in business, consensus decisioning is always a bad thing because it is slow and resource intensive. Consensus decisioning is slower and more resource intensive than the other methods, but it is not something that should be thrown out. There are times when deciding through consensus is the way to go, and sometimes it is the only way to go. The best way to illustrate this is to use a couple examples.

Example: Large business using consensus method

This example comes from a large business with over 5,000 employees globally across 4 business segments. A leadership team was struggling to force a *recommend* decisioning method into the space of enterprise architecture. They needed to make several technology decisions that affected the architecture of their shared systems. Each business segment had a technology representative in the room, and the group struggled with having a single recommender and a single decider because doing so meant that they had to choose someone from one of the groups. Inherently, any individual chosen would have a bias toward their own business segment. They were left with a couple choices to resolve the bias issue: 1) They could add an independent corporate organization that would be neutral to the business segments, or 2) They could pursue a consensus decisioning method. The first approach required adding costs for a new role, something the company did not want to do. With guidance, they decided to implement the second/consensus approach.

Example: Businesses in joint venture using consensus method

This second example comes from two large technology companies who entered a joint venture for product research, design, development, and production. While a joint venture organizational unit was established, there were a couple areas where the companies decided to use their existing resources versus adding additional organizational costs. One of these areas was their business productivity suite. The two separate companies used different business productivity platforms; everything from office software to cloud file storage and team collaboration tools. They needed to make decisions that would not only affect the JV, but the same decisions would also feed back into each respective parent company and have broad-reaching impact with the rest of the enterprise. A single recommender and single decider presented a bias. Since this was viewed as a one-time decision, they did not see the need to add organizational resources to neutralize the bias. Instead, they pursued decision through a team consensus method.

In both these examples, the companies needed to achieve **high quality**, and they were willing to accept a **slower speed** and **higher expenditure** of resources. The line in Table 4 that was referenced in both examples was **H – L – M**. A good quality decision was the primary driving criteria, and the tolerance of a slower speed and higher cost pushes us to the right in the SIDRC/methods graphic in Figure 12. The context of the situations causes us to select *consensus* over *recommend*.

A rigid decision tree is not needed or beneficial when selecting the proper decisioning method. There must be room for us to assess context and select from the methods that are most likely to generate the decision criterion needed for the situation. By allowing ourselves this freedom, we ensure maximum decision effectiveness in our businesses.

8. Decisions Within Processes

Chapter Focus

This chapter examines decisioning in the context of business process management and process mapping. A brief treatment on process mapping is provided so that decision making can be examined in more detail. This sets the stage for the next couple chapters which address how a *group* decisioning process using the *recommend* method functions.

The purpose of all 7 of the performance disciplines is to drive improved business performance in terms of both effectiveness and efficiency. Decisioning and process design both share this goal, and both are highly related disciplines. As a matter fact, process mapping explicitly includes decisions within process flows. Additionally, process mapping helps a team to discover workflow issues, improve quality, diagnose time and resource issues, and identify and eliminate waste.

Focusing on the Diamond

For our purposes of focusing on decision effectiveness in this book, we will not do an exhaustive treatment of process mapping. Instead, we'll provide a quick survey of the basics of process mapping…just enough to give us a launching point to examine the decisioning components.

A process is a series of steps that, when completed, will produce an output. There are different kinds of steps and the type of step is

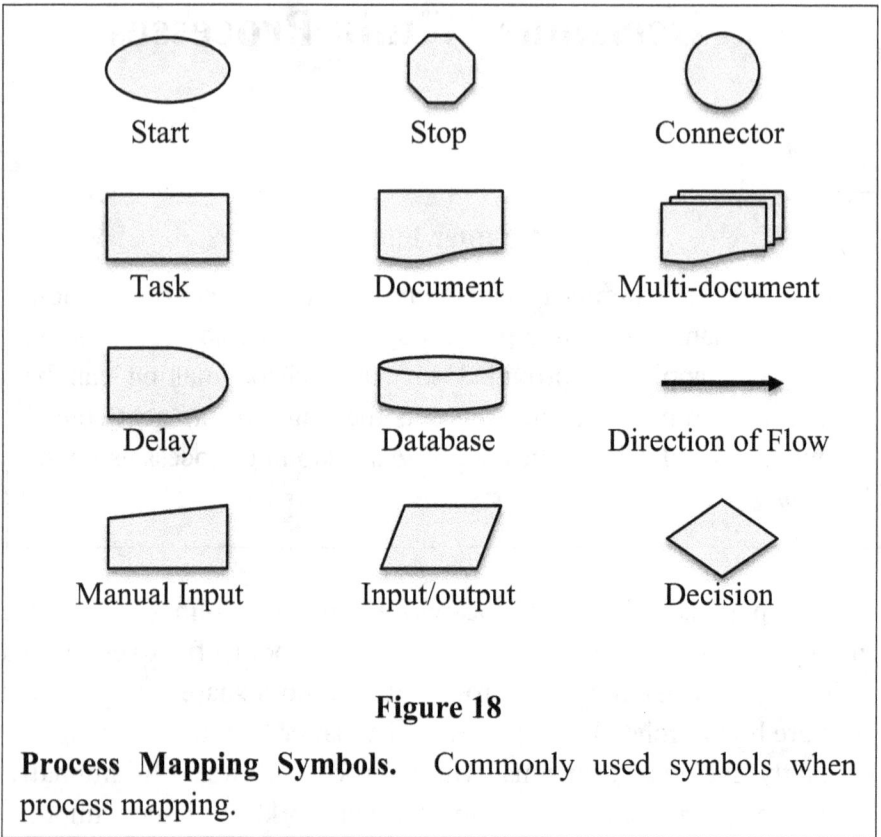

Figure 18

Process Mapping Symbols. Commonly used symbols when process mapping.

represented by a unique symbol. For example, a task is represented by a rectangle and a document is represented by a rectangle with a wave at the bottom. See Figure 18 for common symbology.

The process activity that we are focused on is the decision, and a decision is represented by the diamond, as shown in the bottom-right of Figure 18. It's important to focus on the decision because roles often shift around the decision, and they shift in a way that is commonly overlooked in process mapping. As we learned in an earlier chapter, research has shown that focusing on improving decision-making has significant impact on the performance of the business and the culture. Examining process methodology will help explain why.

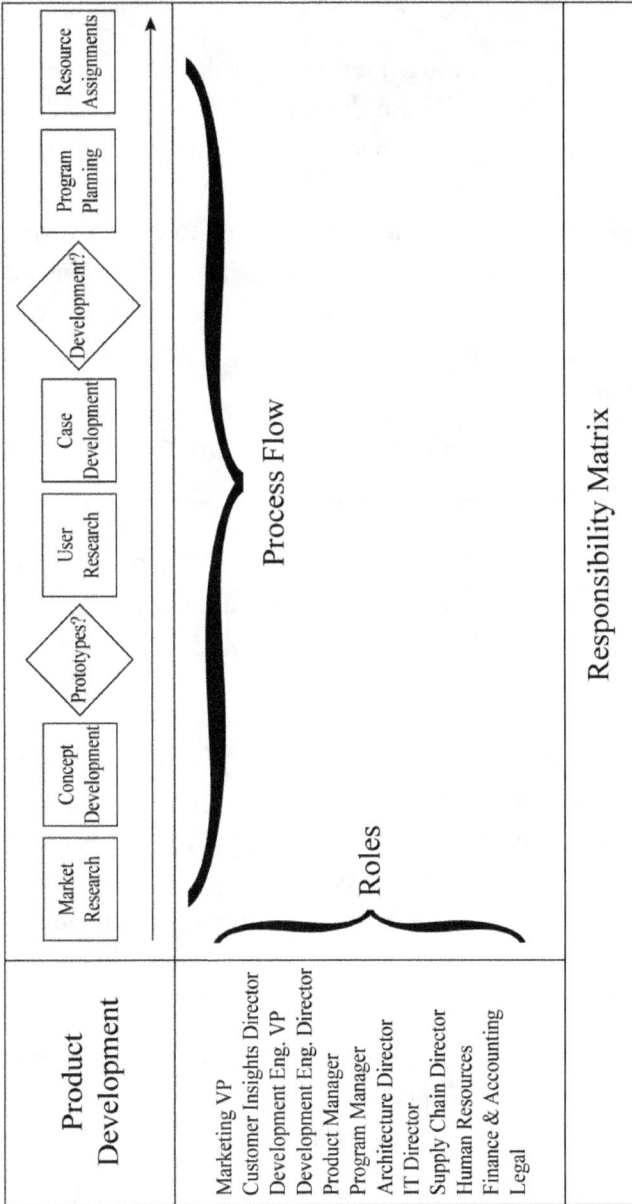

Figure 19

Responsibility Matrix. Example of a responsibility matrix.

Responsibility Matrices

When process mapping, identifying roles often takes the form of responsibility matrices. These matrices are shown as either a separate matrix, accompanying a process flow chart, or they are shown immediately below a process flow chart. A simplified example is in Figure 19. Responsibility matrices are used to clarify responsibilities, streamline resource allocation, ensure task completion, and provide execution consistency between instances of process performance. There are several different names for these types of matrices. Some of the more common ones are:

(RAM) Responsibility Assignment Matrix

(LRC) Linear Responsibility Chart

(RACI) RACI Matrix, where "RACI" stands for the role coding and which will be described later in this chapter.

The rows in the responsibility matrix identify roles, and they're coded using an acronym. We'll get to popular acronyms in a little bit. It's important to emphasize the focus on *roles*. A *role* is a position that is held by one or many people. Roles are used in process mapping to help ensure longitudinal stability of the process maps so they can represent workflow even when people move around in an organization. Compared to using people's names, using roles allows companies to avoid making frequent revisions to processes.

Since responsibility matrices are effectively a sequenced list of actions with role assignments, versions of their use go back a long way into antiquity. Modern use, and the codification of the term RAM, seems to emanate from military use in the 1950's and possibly even used by NASA in the late 1960's. In recent business usage over the past twenty years, RAMs are artifacts that have been predominantly adopted by the program and project management profession.

Prevailing Models for Decision Rights

R.A.C.I.

- Responsible
- Accountable
- Consult
- Inform

Let's start with RACI. Refer to Figure 20. When first used in military and governmental contexts in the 1950's and 1960's, RACI was referred to as a "decision rights matrix." Practitioners of the program and project management (PM) profession may be surprised by this, but RACI did not start as a PM tool. The PM profession was just getting started at that point, as the Project Management Institute (PMI) was founded in 1969, and the first Project Management Book of Knowledge (PMBOK) wasn't published until 1996. RACI actually started as a *decision effectiveness tool.*

One of the things that RACI is supposed to do is provide role clarity (all responsibility matrices seek to improve role clarity.) Unfortunately, RACI has been stretched and redefined so many times through the years that its use can result in the *generation* of *confusion.* In its standard acronym shown above, there's always a degree of confusion between the meanings of "Responsible" and "Accountable." The question often comes up: "Does the *responsible* person do the work or does the *accountable* person do the work?"

To make matters worse, some people substitute the word "Recommend" in place of "Responsible." Others substitute "Assist" in place of "Accountable." *(Sarcastically: I guess if you substitute both out, then nobody's doing any work?)* Then there are extensions to RACI, such as adding a "Support" role and making it RASCI. The quality profession tacks on a Q at the end making it RACI-Q. To try to clear up the confusion between "Responsible" and "Accountable,"

Product Development	Market Research	Concept Development	Prototypes?	User Research	Case Development	Development?	Program Planning	Resource Assignments
Marketing VP	A	R/A	A	R/A	R/A	R/A	C	I
Customer Insights Director	R	C	C	C	I	I	A	A
Development Eng. VP	I	C	R	C	R	R	C	R
Development Eng. Director		I	C	I	C	I	R	R
Product Manager	C	C	C	C	C	I	C	R
Program Manager		I	I		I	I	C	C
Architecture Director			I		I	I	C	C
IT Director			I		I	I	C	C
Supply Chain Director			I		I	I	C	R
Human Resources				I			C	C
Finance & Accounting			I		C	C	C	C
Legal	I		I		I	I	C	C

Responsibility Matrix

Figure 20

Responsibility Matrix with RACI. Sample workflow with RACI coding added for role/responsibility identification.

another adaptation is to drop the "R" and use a "D" in its place to make it DACI, where the "D" stands for "Driver." Much clearer isn't it? Using the previous workflow example, look at Figure 20. Here, RACI coding had been added in a responsibility matrix below the workflow. As an example, look at the first task "Market Research." The Marketing VP is listed as "accountable," and the Customer Insights Director is listed as "responsible." In RACI terminology, this means that the Customer Insights Director is the one who is responsible for completion of the research, and the Marketing VP is ultimately accountable for ensuring that it gets done. Often the roles of "responsible" and "accountable" are in the same line of reporting and the accountability resides with a higher ranking individual than the one performing the work (often, but not always.)

RACI is a good approach for workflow assignments, but it becomes necessary to have multiple parties responsible for accomplishing tasks. When this same coding approach is used for decisions (the diamond,) the decision can end up having multiple responsible. Having multiple people trying to make a decision negatively affects decision quality, speed, level of effort, and outcome. That negative impact is all predicated on a lack of role clarity around the decision itself. As a decision rights model, RACI leaves much to be desired.

D.E.C.I.D.E.

- **D**efine the problem
- **E**stablish criteria
- **C**onsider all the alternatives
- **I**dentify the best alternative
- **D**evelop a plan of action
- **E**valuate and monitor the solution

The DECIDE acronym was built to focus on the decision itself – the diamond in the workflow. This acronym was developed for the healthcare industry. It is intended to help healthcare leaders apply critical thinking to all elements of decision making to generate higher quality decisions. This approach for decision making helps to improve the dimensions of effective decision making by ensuring that participants apply a systematic and rational thought process along with involving the right people. The DECIDE acronym was initially proposed in 2008 by Dr. Kristina Guo.

There are two big challenges with the DECIDE acronym. First, it is difficult to remember. One of the characters, the "D" is repeated, so now we have to also remember that the letter "D" stands for different things. Next, the six characters in DECIDE don't actually stand for six words, they stand for six statements. Because of this, DECIDE is really not an acronym, it is a more general mnemonic. For example, the first "D" stands for "Define the Problem." So, the "D" stands for Define, but if you stop at "Define" we're all left wondering what it is we're supposed to define. So, the "D" really stands for problem, which means it should be a "P" and not a "D." A mnemonic is most powerful as a memory enhancer when it is simple, which is why we prefer actual acronyms, where each letter corresponds very clearly with a single word. You can see where we're heading here; DECIDE is not simple. Second, is that it becomes awkward to implement alongside a process workflow. DECIDE goes beyond roles and responsibilities, it prescribes a process flow within the mnemonic itself. For example, look back at Figure 20. The point of conducting market research is to *define the problem* and *establish success criteria*. In Figure 20, this is addressed through process step and shown in the workflow. However, in the DECIDE mnemonic, the "D" and the "E" stand for defining the problem and establishing success criteria. So, you really can't use DECIDE in a responsibility matrix at all. The same problem repeats with the C and the I. DECIDE is too cumbersome to be used alongside process mapping methodology.

R.A.P.I.D.S.

- **R**ecommendation
- **A**greement
- **P**erformance
- **I**nput
- **D**ecision
- **S**ustain

The RAPIDS acronym is an evolution of an acronym originally proposed by Blenko, et al (2010). While the shorter version of the acronym is trademarked, our expanded version is not. Through this printing we are making the RAPIDS acronym public domain. Please use it, and use it where appropriate for your business. It is a simple and elegant acronym that is easily learned, remembered, and applied…which makes it an excellent mnemonic. To use this version, which is public domain, you must use the Sustain (S) role, which is an expansion of the one originally proposed. You're going to want to use the sustain role anyway, because it solves many issues with implementation, which we'll explain as we go through the rest of the book.

The next chapter on the "Anatomy of a Decision" will examine decision rights in more detail. It's important right now to recall what we learned in the previous chapter about decision methods. From a volume standpoint, the vast majority of the decisions we make do not require group methods or the formality of process. However, when a formal group method and process workflow is needed, it is likely because the business situation requires coordination among a group of people. Consequently, the use of a group *recommend* method, such as the use of the RAPIDS acronym, facilitates the communication of roles and the application of those roles to discrete activities within a process workflow. Let's go over the letters of the acronym and what each of them stands for:

- The "R" stands for "Recommendation": An individual who is coded for this role is the person who orchestrates the rest of the team to produce a formal recommendation for the decision at-hand. A good recommendation considers several different alternatives and presents a business case for each where objective criteria are examined and weighed. Wherever possible, data-driven analyses are conducted, and these are the primary impetus for recommending a course of decision to the decision maker. The person fulfilling the "recommendation" role works with the rest of the team to ensure all forms of input are included. There should be only a single person assigned to the "recommendation" role.

- The "A" stands for "Agreement": An individual who is coded for this role is someone who provides input into a recommendation and whose input is vitally important to the recommended course of action. So important in fact that the Recommender should strive to gain their *agreement* on the recommendation that is made to the decider. Given the gravity of the role, it should be used sparingly and only when necessary. When a team is doing a good job of identifying alternatives to be considered during the creation of a recommendation, it is likely that they will uncover alternatives that will cause this role to issue a disagreement. Disagreement is actually good; it means everyone is doing their job. Hopefully the team can also identify one or more of the alternatives as being acceptable to put forward as a recommendation. If not, a recommendation can go forward where this role disagrees, but it is suggested that the case for disagreement be fully heard by the Decider.

- The "P" stands for "Perform": An individual who is coded for this role is someone who provides input into a recommendation, and their input takes on a very specific form. They are providing input because they will be responsible for performing the execution of the decision once it's made. Therefore, this role should be providing, at a minimum, input regarding what it will take to perform the execution. Things to provide include resource estimates, costs, headcount, and asset requirements.

- The "I" stands for "Input": An individual who is coded for this role is someone who provides input into the consideration of alternatives. Things such as information, analytics, and data are common components of an input.

- The "D" stands for "Decision": An individual who is coded for this role is the person who will make the choice on the course of action. This is the person who has both the accountability and the authority to decide and commit the organization to follow a course of action. If the rest of the process is done well, there's a lot of work that's already taken place. The number one characteristic of a good Decider is that they facilitate discovery. A good decider is inquisitive, seeking to understand the alternatives that are being brought forward and each of their strengths and weaknesses. As much as possible they strive to make data-driven decisions based on a solid business case.

- The "S" stands for "Sustain": An individual who is coded for this role is the person who makes the whole decision method function from end-to-end. Their primary duties include process methodology, workflow integration, team coordination, and communication facilitation. In the acronym's shorter version, there are two common points of failure that exclude a Sustainer role:
  1. The first common point of failure is repeatability. Our work with clients clearly illustrates to us that the ability to apply a chosen decision method and roles requires

someone to own the process workflow. The Sustainer dynamically assesses team involvement and role assignments whenever the process needs to be exercised. This is especially useful in larger organizations and most useful in organizations who use Agile methods for product development. The dynamic team processes associated with Agile sprints mean that the team members and their roles shift and adjust each time the process is exercised. Using a Sustainer role for the process workflow ensures that the roles are all assigned as needed. This successively ensures that high quality recommendations are coming forward with the right speed to produce successful sprint execution.

2. The second common point of failure is decision communications. Commonly, strategic decisions are made a notch or two higher in the organizational structure. At this level of most organizations, Deciders are super-busy. When Deciders are busy, the one thing that suffers is communications. Having someone formally assigned as a Sustainer means that they will *facilitate* the communications needs of the organization. Facilitate is a key word. The Sustainer makes sure that communications are completed both upstream and downstream from the decision, but it is highly suggested that a Decider owns their decision. Afterall, they have both the authority and accountability for their decision, and the organization should be able to rely on them to state what direction was chosen. The Sustainer can act as a facilitator to ensure that this critical step is not overlooked.

We cannot overemphasize the importance of the Sustaining role in the use of RAPIDS. It is this role that makes the acronym agile in its

Product Development	Market Research	Concept Development	Prototypes?	User Research	Case Development	Development?	Program Planning	Resource Assignments
Marketing VP	A	R/A	D	R/A	R/A	R	C	I
Customer Insights Director	R	C	A	C	I			
Development Eng. VP	I	C	R	C	R	D	A	A
Development Eng. Director		I	P	I	C	P	C	R
Product Manager	C	C	P	C	C	P	C	R
Program Manager		I	I/S		I	P/S	R	R
Architecture Director			I		I	I	C	C
IT Director			I		I	I	C	C
Supply Chain Director			I			I	C	C
Human Resources							C	R
Finance & Accounting					C	I	C	C
Legal	I		I	I	I	I	C	C

Responsibility Matrix

Figure 21

Responsibility Matrix with RAPIDS. The RAPIDS acronym is shown in the workflow under both decisions (diamonds) shown in the workflow.

application. It is this role that helps to ensure change-leadership and a consistent execution of the decision method.

For an illustration of the use of RAPIDS inside the context of workflow, refer to Figure 21. In the figure, we have used the same process workflow illustrated previously. The new RAPIDS acronym has been applied to the decision (diamond) in the workflow. Using this acronym allows us to very clearly identify who the decider is, who the recommender is, and the roles that the others play in the decisioning process. There is a little more refining that can be done to this workflow; let's look at that next.

Steps Surrounding a Decision

There are two steps that in-practice have proven to be invaluable when applying the decision role acronym. Wherever there is a decision (diamond) in a process flow, add a step before it for "Preparing the Recommendation," and then add a step after it for "Communicating the Decision." Figure 22 shows this change in the process workflow for the previous example.

The two steps have been added, one on each side of the decision (diamond.) The RAPIDS acronym is applied to the responsibility matrix in the preparation of a recommendation, the decision itself, and the follow-on communication. Once the decision-communication is completed, the RACI acronym continues and is used for the successive steps in the process flow. In practice, these three steps become critical to providing the maximum amount of role clarity and gaining the most leverage out of using both RACI and RAPIDS acronyms together.

Using the acronyms and process workflow in this manner, it becomes visually clear who is participating in the recommendation preparation, who is participating in the decisioning, and who is responsible for decision communications. The decisioning is highly streamlined and ideally involves only one decision maker and one person presenting a recommendation. The rest of the roles are

Product Development	Market Research	Concept Development	Prepare Recommendation	Prototypes?	Communicate Decision	User Research
Marketing VP	A	R/A	A	D	P/A	R/A
Customer Insights Director	R	C				C
Development Eng. VP	I	C	R	R	I	C
Development Eng. Director		I	P			I
Product Manager	C	C	P			C
Program Manager		I	I/S	S	P/S	
Architecture Director			I			
IT Director			I			
Supply Chain Director			I			
Human Resources						
Finance & Accounting						
Legal	I		I			
Responsibility Matrix	RACI	RACI	RAPIDS	RAPIDS		RACI

Figure 22

Responsibility Matrix with Two Acronyms. Workflow showing the addition of two tasks around the decision and the application of a second acronym to improve role clarity.

participating in building the recommendation and they receive information about the decision after it has been made. There are some additional rules to the roles, and there are certainly exceptions that can be made. These will be covered in the next chapter where we will examine the anatomy of the decision.

Summary

Responsibility matrices are put in place to provide clarity on roles and responsibilities. Using the right acronym enhances clarity in the business. The opposite is true too, using the wrong acronyms can create confusion. Sometimes certain acronyms are difficult to remember and apply. But, there is a need to drive improved clarity around decisioning. Modifying the responsibility matrix and using two different acronyms for coding responsibilities is an excellent way to provide the clarity that organizations need. This is a great way to improve process workflows and has been tested in application.

9. Mapping Decision Rights

Chapter Focus

This chapter explains how to map decision rights and how to move from current state to future state. It explores some of the more common issues encountered along the way and how to mitigate them. It also further explains how and when to apply the different acronyms, such as RACI, to decisions.

Remember from an earlier chapter that the assignment of decision rights is about putting organizational power in the right place. When organizational power is wielded in the right way we can generate success and maximize decision effectiveness. Our focus of this book is on driving business performance improvement while leveraging decision effectiveness as one of the disciplines to help us do that.

To use decision authority and autonomy (power) in a way that benefits and optimizes the business, leaders will regularly need to ensure that decision authority is placed with the _roles_ that are best positioned to make an effective decision. Doing so helps to ensure that the source of power is primarily **positional** and secondarily **expert**. When we intentionally align decision making authority and autonomy in this way we are saying that the decision belongs here because:

- This _role_ is in the best place to make the choice for the business
- Anyone who occupies this _role_ will have the information they need
- They will see the data that supports the decision and best understand its implications on performance

- Any lower in the organization and the picture will be incomplete
- Any higher in the organization and the role will be too far removed from relevant detail, context, and information

Decision rights are all about the above five bullet points and getting them correct. The work starts by fully defining and vetting the decisions themselves. Once the decision are defined, then the decision rights and roles can be identified. It's useful to reemphasize points made in earlier chapters. For those decisions that use the more individual methods of *solo*, *inform*, and *discuss*, it's unnecessary to map decision rights. In situations where these decision show up in process workflows, it is fine to leave them coded with an acronym like RACI. However, for those decisions that require a group method such as *recommend* or *consensus*, the use of RAPIDS to clarify roles and responsibilities is valuable. We will examine the mapping of decision rights from the perspective of the *recommend* method; subsequently we will briefly review how to extend this into the *consensus* method when needed.

Writing Decisions

The first step to mapping decision rights is identifying and writing a decision. It's a bigger task than you might initially think, and it's often one that benefits greatly from facilitation by a third party. The challenge is getting the group to clearly articulate decisions, sequence them successively in a workflow. Once that's done, then the work of applying decision rights to those decisions can be completed. Again, the decision rights activity is based on the need for a group-based *recommend* methodology. This last point is very important to highlight. Accomplishing group agreement on decision rights requires work and resources. If you think back to the number of decisions we all make in a day (35,000) and do some "back of the napkin" extrapolations to estimate the number of decisions made in your organization…then take a percentage of those that are "important."

Well, you still end up with a very high number of decisions. The reality is that in our businesses we make most of our decisions using the *solo, inform,* and *discuss* methods. One of the biggest advantages to the information age is that we can access the information that we need whenever we need it. This information access facilitates a higher degree of *solo* and *inform* decision making.

Group effort in decision mapping should be on those decisions that we need to align on. These are decisions that you might label as "key" or "critical." They may also be decisions that simply don't work well today where you have organizational misalignment, conflict, or they're just plain weird. Going through a decision rights mapping exercise is a highly effective way of promoting healthy conflict and problem solving.

When writing a decision, usually the first thing to come up is a category and not an actual decision. For example, the first expression of a decision might be, "business initiatives." Or, another common expression would be "who makes the decision about our business initiative?" Reworded, it could take the form of:

What are the prioritized business initiatives for the company?

Here's an example from marketing. A first expression might be, "trade shows for the year." Reworded, it could take the form of:

What is our event calendar for the year?

Here's an example from sales. A first expression might be, "account list per sales rep." Reworded, it could take the form of:

What is the account assignment per territory for each sales representative?

This third example is from human resources. A first expression might be, "selecting the candidate to hire." Reworded, it could take the form of:

Who, within a candidate pool, who is selected to receive an offer?

When decisions are written, they are best phrased as questions. You might be thinking that a decision is about making a choice or declaring which direction we're going to go, so why would we word them as questions? It's true that a decision is a choice or declaration. Reminder that we're focused on the *recommend* method of decision making; therefore, the declaration is the <u>outcome</u> of a set of work activities involving other people. While the decider does make a declaration, everyone else on the team works toward answering a question, providing input, performing analyses, understanding alternatives, and preparing a *recommendation*. Even in the case of the decider, 99% of the Decider's time is spent (should be) exploring the alternatives, understanding data and analytics, and facilitating group discussion. A miniscule amount of time is spent making the declaration. People will rally around questions; not so much around declarations.

Most commonly the questions will start with the word "what." Let's briefly examine the use of each of the pronouns that could be used to start a decision. "What" and "Who" are the most often used words, followed by "When" and "Where":

What:

First and foremost, there is tremendous value in consistency. You will find that most decisions can be started with the word "what." From experience, *most* meaning about 80% (following the 80/20 rule.) Using the word "what" is the easiest pronoun to use because it naturally allows the team to think through the roles that will participate in the decisioning process. All of the other pronouns will risk leading people to either declarations or an insufficient definition of roles.

Who:

The use of the word "who" is a common one to see when teams first start to practice decision effectiveness. It takes the form of

"Who will make the decision about...." If you use the word "who" in this way, you will only ever identify the decider, and the rest of the roles that need to participate will be missed. Consequently, the decisioning process will suffer and you will put at-risk decision quality and effort. The only time that a decision should start with the word "who" is if that decision is about making a choice among people.

The previous example from human resources is relevant here. That decision was about selecting one candidate from a pool of candidates who would receive a job offer. In this case the decision is a person selection. Worded as a "who" question, it would look like this: "Who among the candidates will receive a job offer?" Even in this case, it is advisable to re-word the decision to use the word "what" because it will avoid confusion. Rewording it in this manner might look like this: "What candidate will be selected to receive a job offer?"

For another example, let's say you must decide who attends the company's annual sales meeting. First inclination might be worded like this "Who decides the sales meeting attendees?" Again, in this case all we will determine is who the decider is, when what we want is to determine the attendee list. Reworded it would be, "Who are the attendees for the national sales meeting?" Even this decision can be re-worded using the word "what": "What is the attendee list for the national sales meeting?"

Again, consistency matters a lot, and it is best to guide people to use the pronoun "what" as often as possible. The "who" pronoun is the most problematic of the four.

When:

The use of the word "when" is less common, and it's usually a little easier to get teams to reword these using the word "what." An example is, "When will the quarterly sales review meetings be held?" Another is, "When are we going to hold our annual strategic planning meeting?" Both of these <u>are good ways</u> to word a decision. Frankly, it's hard to get into trouble with this pronoun from a decision-wording standpoint. However, in this case it is still advisable to push teams to start with the pronoun "what." Both decisions are easily reworded this way:

"What's the quarterly sales review schedule for the year?"

"What's the strategic planning calendar for the year?"

While it's advisable for consistency purposes to have teams reword their decisions using the pronoun "what," in this case the use of the word "when" is acceptable.

Where:

The use of the word "where" is even less common, and it's equally easy to reword using the word "what." An example is, "Where will we locate the new data center?" Another is, "Where will we hold the company's annual product exposition?" Both of these <u>are good ways to word</u> decisions. It's hard to get into trouble with this pronoun too; however, it's still advisable to coach teams to reword using the pronoun "what." These could easily be reworded as:

"What is the location of the new data center?"

"What will the location be for the product exposition?"

The reason you want to guide teams to use the pronoun "what" is that it keeps the rules simple and straightforward. When something is easy to remember, it's easier to apply. Two simple rules for writing decisions which will help teams move more quickly through decision writing:

1. Write decisions as questions

2. Start with the word "what"

Hiring a New Position	Discuss		Recommend				
Decision Methods	Phone Screening	What is the interviewing team?	Interviews	Recommendation for hiring	What candidate will receive an offer?	Communicate Decision	Extend Offer
HR Vice President		I	I	I			I
HR Rewards Director			I				C
HR Recruiting Director	A	I	I	I			C
Legal				I			I
Hiring Manager +1	I	C	R	I	D		I
Hiring Manager	I	C	R	R	R	I	A
HR Business Partner		R	R	A			C
Recruiter	R	A	A	P/S	S	P/S	R
Interviewer 1		I	R	I			I
Interviewer 2		I	R	I			I
Interviewer 3		I	R	I			I
Interviewer(s)			R	I			I
Responsibility Matrix	RACI			RAPIDS		RACI	

Figure 23

Hiring Workflow and Decisions. Illustrates a portion of a hiring workflow, identification of decision method, and the application of different acronyms for the responsibility matrix.

Selecting the Decision Method

It's important to understand decision placement in workflow and what decision method needs to be used, prior to mapping decision rights. Refer to Figure 23 for an example which depicts a portion of a hiring process for a new position in a company. The workflow is presented normally using standard process mapping symbology and RACI for the responsibility matrix. There are two decisions listed:

What is the interviewing team?

What candidate will receive an offer?

The decision methods chosen for each decision are listed above the process flow. Remember the five methods available: *Solo, Inform, Discuss, Recommend,* and *Consensus.*

For the first decision, *discuss* is the method chosen. This means that the company is expressing the want/need to have a *discussion* about who comprises the interviewing team. The position that will ensure that this *discussion* occurs is the one coded as *responsible,* or the Human Resources Business Partner. Since the Recruiter is an integral part of the entire process, their role is significant throughout, and in the first decision they hold the *accountability* role – to ensure that this step gets completed. The others who would be in the *discussion* include those labeled as *consult,* which are the Hiring Manager and the Hiring Manager's boss (Hiring Manager +1). Using the *discuss* method means that the HR Business Partner is the person who will make the decision about who's on the interviewing team, but they will do this with *discussion-based-input* from those identified. No formal *recommendation* process is needed.

For the second decision, *recommend* is the method chosen. This means that the company is expressing the want/need to have a formal *recommendation* come forward to the *decider.* Since this decision is a *recommendation* method, the acronym used in the responsibility matrix changes to RAPIDS which is a recommendation-based approach for coding decision roles.

A recommendation is a team activity that is performed in order to identify alternatives, weigh the pros and cons of each, and suggest a best course of action. The position that will facilitate the recommendation activity is the Hiring Manager, and the Decider is the Hiring Manager's boss (Hiring Manager +1). The team involved in creating the recommendation is extensive and includes almost everyone on the list. Most are inputs. In the RAPIDS acronym the "I" stands for input; whereas, in the RACI acronym the "I" stands for inform. In the RAPIDS framework, all roles fulfilled are active roles; *all roles have material contribution.* In contrast, the inform role in RACI is a passive role, where the people coded with this role simply need to be made aware of what's going on.

For the hiring recommendation, eight people have material input. Half of those were active participants in the interviewing process. The other half possess key information about the applicants that has been acquired through the recruiting process. The HR Business Partner is coded as an "A" for *agree*, meaning that they must agree with the *recommendation* before it is presented to the decider. If the HR Business Partner does not agree with the recommendation, the decider should hear the disagreement and the reasons why. The Recruiter is coded as a "P" and "S" for *perform* and *sustain.* The Recruiter is in the perform role because they have material input and because they must execute the work after the decision is made; hence the Recruiter's subsequent coding as an "R" for the extend offer step (where RACI coding is continued). The Recruiter is in the sustain role because they are in the best position to ensure that the decision process and rights are implemented as desired by the company, and they are in the best position to facilitate decision-communications once the decision is rendered.

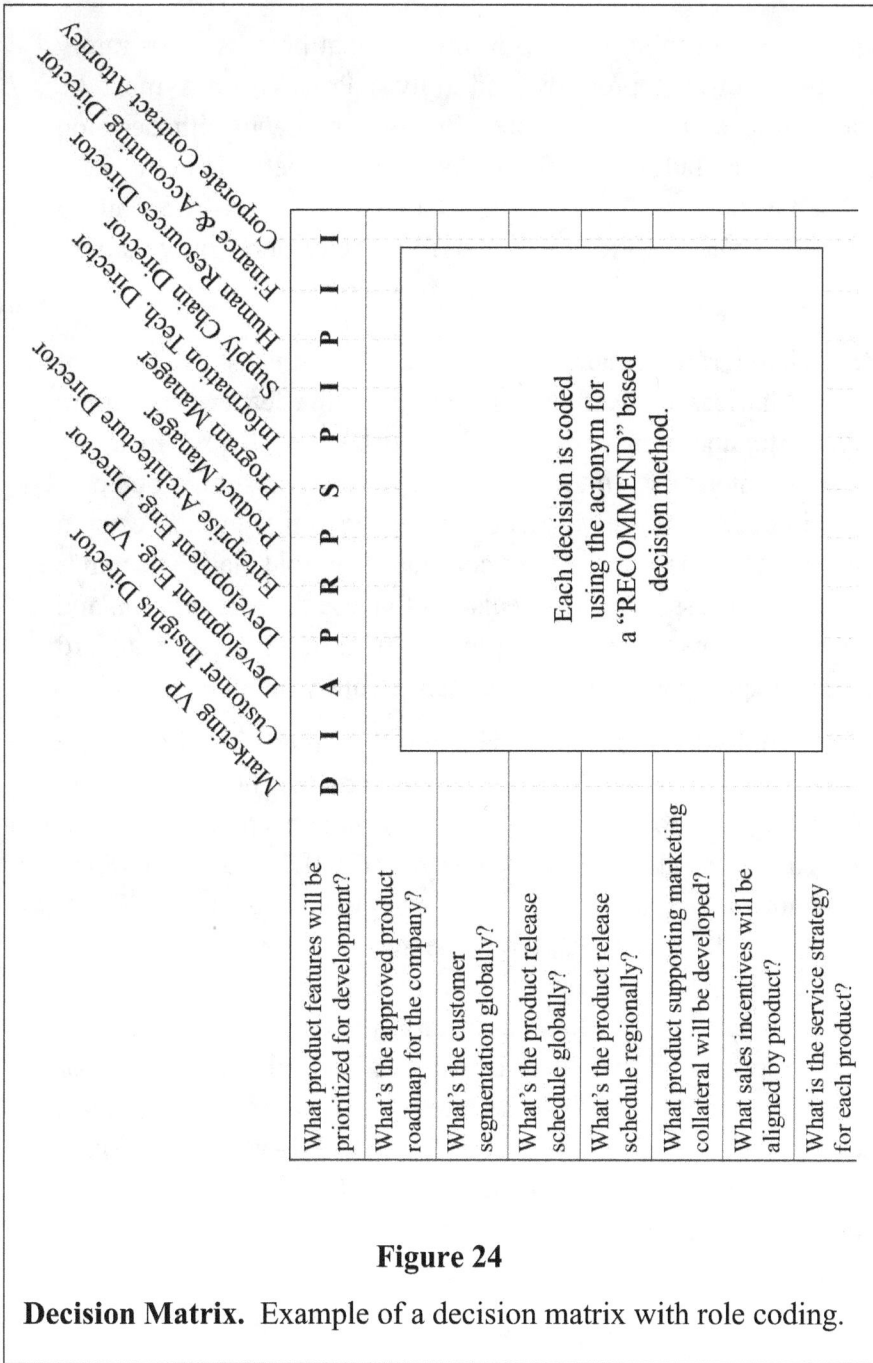

	Marketing VP	Customer Insights Director	Development Insights Director	Development Eng. VP	Enterprise Architecture Director	Product Manager	Program Manager	Information Tech. Director	Supply Chain Director	Human Resources Director	Finance & Accounting Director	Corporate Contact Attorney
	D	I	A	P	R	P	S	P	I	P	I	I
What product features will be prioritized for development?												
What's the approved product roadmap for the company?												
What's the customer segmentation globally?												
What's the product release schedule globally?												
What's the product release schedule regionally?												
What product supporting marketing collateral will be developed?												
What sales incentives will be aligned by product?												
What is the service strategy for each product?												

Each decision is coded using the acronym for a "RECOMMEND" based decision method.

Figure 24

Decision Matrix. Example of a decision matrix with role coding.

One important thing to keep in mind is that process maps rarely express the decisions properly and fully. Process maps must be modified to accommodate a more effective approach with decision making. This includes identifying the decision methods along with extending the process flow with a set of consistent tasks around a decision and switching the acronym used in the responsibility matrix.

Decision Rights Matrices

A decision rights matrix is essentially a spreadsheet view of decisions. Matrices are useful when working with a leadership team to identify, write, and assign roles to "key" decisions. "Key" meaning that these decisions use either the *recommend* or *consensus* methods. They are important or weighty enough decisions that group decision methods must be applied to them; consequently, role clarity becomes paramount to success. Usually, decisions that use the *solo*, *inform*, and *discuss* methods can remain in process workflows using standard process language, such as RACI, for responsibility matrices.

An example decision matrix is shown in Figure 24. Typically, decisions are written in rows on the left side, and the roles are listed in columns along the top. The matrix itself is coded using the letters of the acronym you've chosen. The acronyms DECIDE and RAPIDS are most common. (For reasons previously mentioned about the DECIDE mnemonic, we'll continue through the rest of the book using the acronym RAPIDS.) In this matrix you can see how each decision starts with the pronoun "what," and each decision is clearly and succinctly worded. Keep in mind that every decision exists within the context of a workflow and there will likely be other things impacted by changes in decision rights. We will review these additional impacts in a subsequent chapter on change management. Here are some tips for a good decision matrix:

- Include decisions that are "key," meaning they require a higher level of group involvement and use either the *recommend* or *consensus* methods.
- Sequence the decisions from top to bottom so they follow the progression of workflow through the organization's value chain.
- Sequence the roles from left to right so they follow the organizational hierarchy.
- Doing the prior two bullets allows you to see how the decision and recommendation responsibilities flow through the organization. If you are empowering your workforce, you will see the decision and recommendation coding move down and to the right in the matrix.
- Color coding is very useful for a "live" matrix. Use a consistent color key in your organization so people can quickly identify the roles. *(Hard to do in a printed book without doubling the price of the book...sorry.)*

Extending into the Consensus Method

Since the consensus method is a group method, all that has been presented as part of the *recommend* method can be used in the *consensus* method. Refer to Figure 25. In-effect, the process associated with the *recommend* method is multiplied by the number of constituents, and the *Sustain* role in RAPIDS takes on an even greater significance.

Within a single constituency, the workflow associated with preparing a recommendation functions exactly the same as it does under the recommend method. The group of recommender, input(s), agree(s), and perform(s) work together to construct alternatives, examine business cases, and prepare a recommendation. This activity is conducted in each of the constituencies.

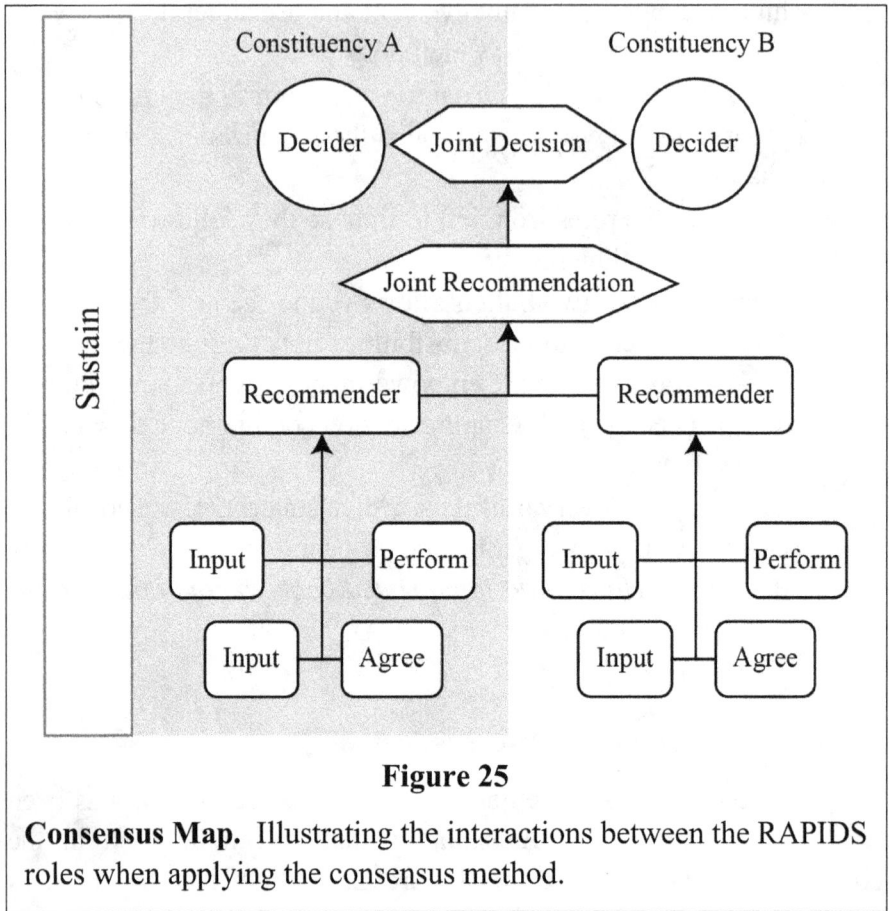

Figure 25

Consensus Map. Illustrating the interactions between the RAPIDS roles when applying the consensus method.

When all the constituencies are ready with their respective recommendations (and underlying alternatives,) the recommenders come together. Their *ideal* goal is to construct a joint-recommendation. They go through a process of sharing their recommendations, discussing their business cases, and supporting information. Preparing a joint recommendation is a highly iterative set of working sessions. The teams may need to explore alternatives, and they may need to break apart their alternatives and re-examine underlying requirements.

For the deciders, in the best-case what comes forward is a joint recommendation. If this has been achieved, the decision-making may be much easier and faster. In either case, the deciders should go through a consideration process where they ask the recommenders to present the issue, recommendation, alternatives considered, and their rationale for the recommendation. There are several outcomes that can occur, and these are listed below in order of their likelihood:

- Push the recommendation down for rework. The deciders hear the recommendation(s) and request that the team(s) go back into working sessions to examine/adjust some of the content. This results in a follow-on presentation of the revised recommendation.
- Approval. The deciders hear a joint-recommendation and approve it to move forward. It's common that approval is granted as conditional and pending some requested changes.
- All recommendations are voted-down and there's an impasse. This one is unfortunate, but it happens more than it probably should. It in-effect means that the constituencies are unwilling or unable to move toward each other through agreeable concessions. This results in fewer approvals than is necessary to carry a decision forward and the process stalls. Most common in government.
- Deciders opt to work out their own solution. The deciders have heard the recommendation(s) and alternative(s), and they have chosen as a group to assemble an alternative solution that was not seen or presented by the team(s). The smaller a business is, the more common this outcome.

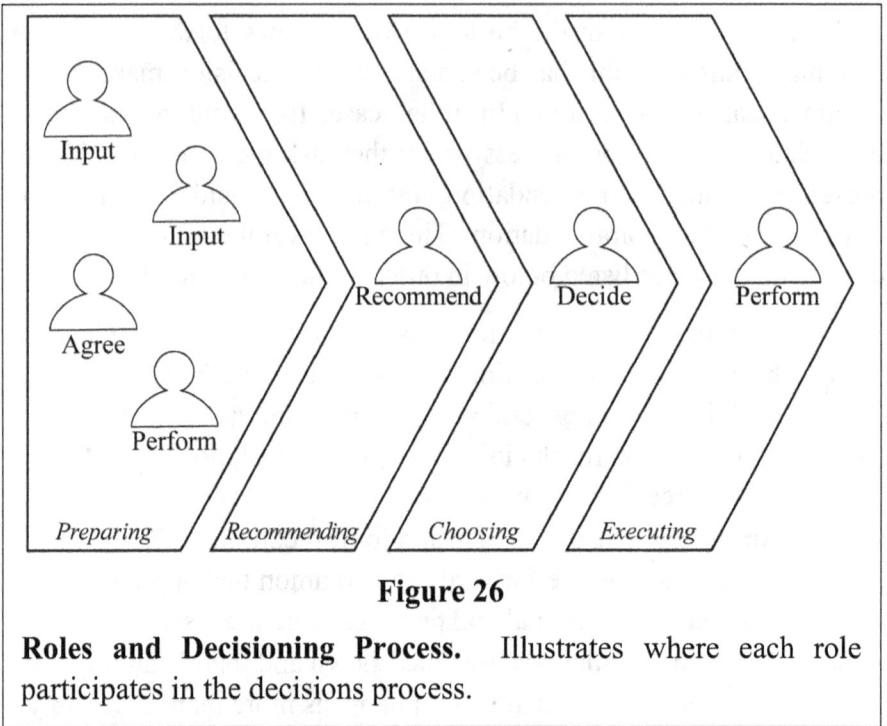

Figure 26

Roles and Decisioning Process. Illustrates where each role participates in the decisions process.

The sustain role continues as a facilitator. This is the same role that was presented in the recommend method; however, in the consensus method the sustain role is vital for an effective interaction when recommendations are brought forward for discussion with the deciders. The person in the sustain role should take an unbiased and neutral position, where their goal is to ensure that the process keeps moving forward and that the teams have productive engagements.

Summary

Of the five decision methods, using the *recommend* and *consensus* methods requires the most training and practice. Once people have acquired some initial training and skill with decision effectiveness and the definition of decision rights, the biggest misconception that continues is an over-focus on the *decider*. Refer to Figure 26. When these methods are executed well, the central point of focus in the decisioning process is actually the *recommender* and the *team* that helps to put together well-vetted recommendations. Without a well-functioning team, the recommender is "dead in the water" and is forced back into a more individualistic method most likely resembling the *discuss* method.

Popular op-eds make this over-focus on the decider even more pronounced. Popular psychology and self-help books are geared toward the more individualistic methods of *solo*, *inform*, and *discuss* to improve your personal decision making. They largely seek to help you improve your personal decision making. Do a quick book search on 'decision making' using your favorite on-line book retailer. The overwhelming majority of the books are oriented to individual decision making. As business leaders, we help lead our organizations through decision making. Organizational decision effectiveness, on key decisions, relies on *teamwork*. In contrast to individual approaches, *organizational* decision effectiveness seeks to help us improve our collective decision making which will in-turn enable us to drive improved business performance. A big difference! Effective decision making will clearly identify roles. The right team, applied at the right time, will generate quality recommendations that are both timely, of high-quality, and resource efficient.

10. Measuring Decision Effectiveness

Chapter Focus

This chapter gives you a first-look at how your organization does with decision effectiveness. It presents you with a short series of questions that you can use to quickly gauge decision effectiveness. Then the chapter concludes with some cautions regarding other available indices and benchmarks.

If we want decision effectiveness to improve, we need to measure how we're doing. As the saying goes, 'anything worth doing is worth measuring.' And, there's an equally relevant one that says, 'inspect what you expect.' In other words, if you measure it you're much more likely to receive it.

Rate Your Organization

When we conduct employee surveys we develop deep and accurate measurements which are filtered by subsidiary, organizational unit, department, geography, function, and level. It's vitally important to be able to filter survey results by each of your organizational dimensions. Use Tables 5 and 6 to perform a quick rating on decision effectiveness for your organization. The worksheets presented in Tables 5 and 6 are a *preliminary* and *qualitative* view. What you come up with for a grade is intended to give you a "sense of things."

When conducting employee surveys on this subject it's important to collect information *broadly* across the organization and *deeply* throughout the organization. Insights depend on a couple key points.

Rate the following 5 questions then average the score:	1	2	3	4	5	6	7	8	9	10
	Strongly Disagree									*Strongly Agree*
Decisions are made at the right speed.								8		
After decisions are made, we feel good about the quality of our decisions.							7			
We spend the right amount of effort to make decisions.						6				
Once we decide, we are satisfied with the results of our work.									9	
I have the right amount of decision-authority to do my job effectively.					5					

Total Points from Above: _____ 35

Divide by 5 to get an Average: _____ 7

Our employees understand who to go to for key decisions.	Yes	0.80	Multiply by your answer to this question...
	Maybe	0.70	0.70
	No	0.60	

Resultant Quotient: _____ 4.9

Our employees understand what decisions are made and why.	Yes	+0.20	Add to your answer to this question...
	Maybe	-0.10	+0.20
	No	-0.20	

Resultant Quotient: _____ 6.9

Look up your grade in this chart:

≤ 5.9	6.0 – 6.9	7.0 – 7.9	8.0 – 8.9	9.0 – 9.9
F	D	C	B	A

Table 5

Example Rating. An example using the rating worksheet provided in Table 6.

Rate the following 5 questions then average the score:	1	2	3	4	5	6	7	8	9	10
	Strongly Disagree									*Strongly Agree*
Decisions are made at the right speed.										
After decisions are made, we feel good about the quality of our decisions.										
We spend the right amount of effort to make decisions.										
Once we decide, we are satisfied with the results of our work.										
I have the right amount of decision-authority to do my job effectively.										

Total Points from Above: _____

Divide by 5 to get an Average: _____

Our employees understand who to go to for key decisions.	Yes	0.80	Multiply by your answer to this question…
	Maybe	0.70	
	No	0.60	

Resultant Quotient: _____

Our employees understand what decisions are made and why.	Yes	+0.20	Add to your answer to this question…
	Maybe	-0.10	
	No	-0.20	

Resultant Quotient: _____

Look up your grade in this chart:

≤ 5.9	6.0 – 6.9	7.0 – 7.9	8.0 – 8.9	9.0 – 9.9
F	**D**	**C**	**B**	**A**

Table 6

Rating Your Organization. A short worksheet to determine a preliminary rating for decision effectiveness.

First is that *all* your employees matter when collecting insights. We often hear from leaders that they don't want to survey a certain segment of their employee population, many times pointing to their hourly population. We push back on this because of a concept known as "sphere of knowledge and influence."

Sphere of knowledge and influence is a simple concept which means that every person has a finite degree of interactions, knowledge, and influence over their surroundings. These interactions include work tasks, the physical environment, social structures, and economic transactions, to name a few. As Figure 27 depicts, an individual's knowledge and influence are highest closest to them. Each degree of separation that you move away from the individual, the amount of knowledge and influence reduces in a proportionate manner.

If one restricts surveying, the information that's collected only extends to the sphere of knowledge and influence of the population surveyed. Restrict the survey to say your top 3 layers, and at-best the information collected represents what's going on at layer three and *maybe* layer four. The only reason that one might take this approach is if you believed there were no decision effectiveness issues lower in the organization. That belief would be a bit unrealistic. Likewise, it is vitally important that whenever surveying is done, that you have the ability to filter and sort the data by organizational dimension. Decision effectiveness data is especially sensitive to where someone is placed in the organization, the type of work that they do, and their interactions with systems, processes, tools, and people. Being able to explore the data generates the most useful insights and makes them *actionable*.

The second key point is that proper sampling improves accuracy. This is certainly no secret in the world of data analytics, and yet it's still very important to emphasize. Adequate sampling helps to ensure high confidence levels in the data through a *representative* data collection processes. Like all other types of surveying, it is virtually impossible to reach the entire population within normal time and

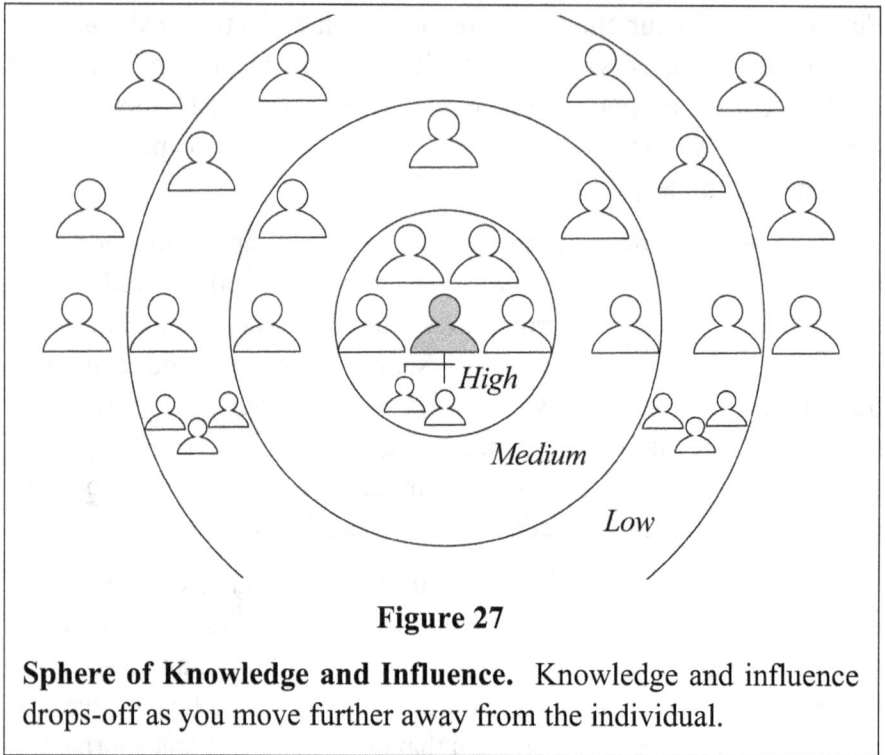

Figure 27

Sphere of Knowledge and Influence. Knowledge and influence drops-off as you move further away from the individual.

budget constraints. So, when conducting surveys, we seek to collect input from a smaller (and representative) sample of the total population. The greater the percent of sample, the more accurately the results *represent* the views of the whole population. If you can pull it off, it's always better to collect everyone's input; absent that possibility, sampling *reflects* the population.

Let's come back to Tables 5 and 6 for a minute. These worksheets are here to provide you a quick way to do a preliminary review of what *you believe* decision effectiveness is like in your organization. The resulting grade is one person's opinion…yours. It is not a representative sample. Use the worksheets as a barometer, or an early detection gauge, to help you figure out if you need to further measure your organization's decision effectiveness. If you score poorly on these

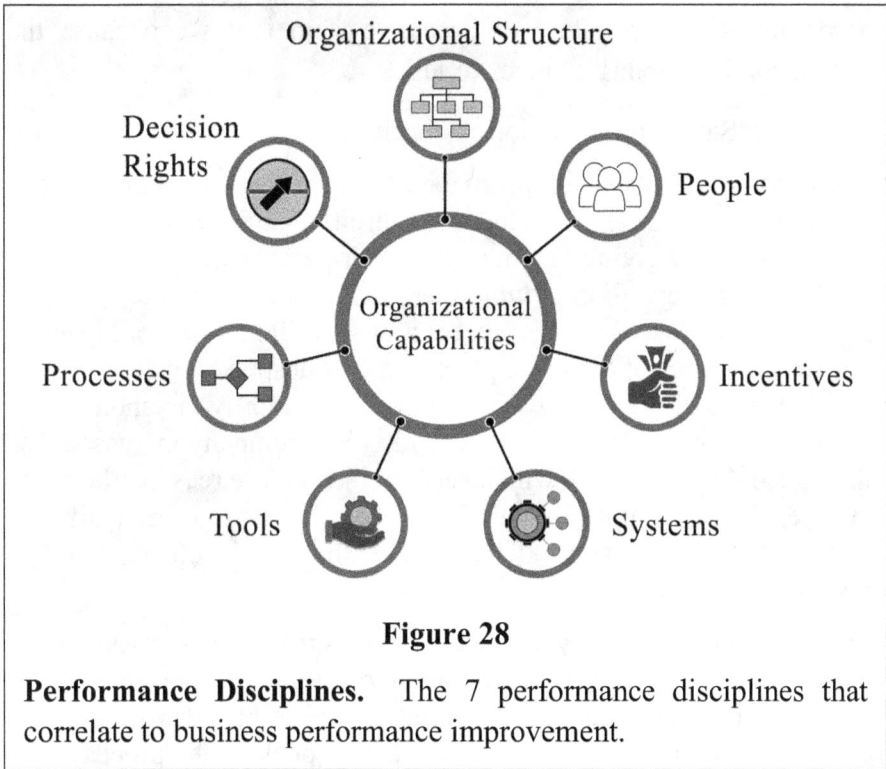

Figure 28

Performance Disciplines. The 7 performance disciplines that correlate to business performance improvement.

worksheets, you will want to examine decision effectiveness more thoroughly.

When measuring decision effectiveness, it is important to do so in the context of the other performance disciplines. Recall from an earlier chapter that any one of the performance disciplines, shown again in Figure 28, *slightly* correlates to improved performance. But, when they are combined, the combination is accretive and drives improved performance. Measuring the dimensions of decision effectiveness (e.g. clarity, quality, speed, effort, yield, empowerment, etc.) should be done in context of the other 6 disciplines because it is highly likely that an identified weakness in decisioning scores has parallel needs. For example, solving for role clarity on decision rights while *not* solving for organizational structure or process/system issues can cause the subsequent decisioning changes to fail.

> Example: Salesforce Decision Authorities
>
> A company was trying to improve its outside sales interactions with customers. The issue presented itself through the sales force, which was consistently giving feedback that their performance was limited by their decision authority, which was tied to the size of the customer sale/deal. In this case, for a multi-billion-dollar company with a sales force of over 500 people, each salesperson's decision authority was set at $5,000. These decision authority thresholds had not been reviewed in over a decade. The company increased the threshold to $50,000, which seemed like a more reasonable number. Seems simple enough, but there was a lot of other work that went with the change. This included three of the other disciplines:
>
> Processes: The company had intricate sales review processes in place. Management reviewed potential deals and the deal review process had in intricate web of escalations based on a deal's projected revenue potential and scope. This deal review process needed to be redefined along with all the review thresholds because the 10-fold increase in salesperson authority meant that most of the sales review meetings would go away.
>
> Tools: To give the salespeople a 10X authority increase, the leadership team required more thorough business cases. Each salesperson would now be required to have complete client portfolios, and financial analyses. Historically, the deal review structure functioned as a stop-gap measure to ensure a thorough understanding of risk. Now that the salesperson was assuming the authority and accountability for a 10X revenue decision, the salesperson would need to do a more exhaustive treatment on prospective customers to ensure decision quality.
>
> Systems: There were systems implications to the company's salesforce automation and enterprise resource planning systems. Routing and authority tables needed to be reconfigured to match the

new decision authority levels and workflow requirements. Without these system changes the work orders would continue to follow the "old way."

These changes did not occur all at one time either. The company applied formal charters to define the change projects, assigned project leaders, leadership sponsors, project managers, and the necessary resources for execution. The company went through a change process that took several weeks to complete and included formal communications and training for the salesforce. In the end, it was successful!

Had any one of these pieces been skipped/missed, the entire effort could have been at risk of failure. The 7 disciplines work together to generate business performance improvements. You likely will not need to invoke all seven all the time, but you will need to use two or more on a regular basis to drive performance improvement.

Indices and Benchmarks

Since this is a chapter on the measurement of decision effectiveness, it's worth a final word on indices and benchmarks. We're big fans of indices and benchmarks...where they make sense. An example of beneficial benchmarks is employee engagement, and another one is in the dimensions of company culture. In the area of decision effectiveness, we are not fans of benchmarks. Let us explain why.

Ratings on decision effectiveness are highly contextual. The dimensions of decision effectiveness depend on many variables including products, services, mix, markets, differentiation, pricing, and more. To further contextualize, add in higher-level governing variables such as industry, industry sub-segment, country, and geography. Then, couple these variables with the mix of decision measurement dimensions including roles, quality, speed, effort, yield, and empowerment. It quickly becomes evident how much variation there can be. Decision effectiveness is highly contextual. Even trying to compare your company against your closest competitor (if it were possible) is still not beneficial. Against your closest competition, you will (should) have different approaches to product/service mix and differentiation. Those strategic business differences drive *your* organization's decision making.

FAR more useful is an internal benchmark of sorts, where you can view changes in decisioning over time…longitudinal internal benchmarking is <u>*highly valuable*</u>. Being able to see changes in the decisioning dimensions as you implement initiatives, make organization structure adjustments, and change leadership talent enables you to proactively tune the organization for maximum performance. When combined with all 7 performance disciplines, the ratings/metrics represent your company's unique fingerprint.

Leverage a Powerful Employee Survey

Imagine having the insights about all seven of these areas: organization structure, decision effectiveness, process design, systems, tools, incentives, and people as you roll-out initiatives, adjust your organization, and leverage talent. These types of insights are always *actionable*. So many employee surveys fail to deliver follow-up actions because they are not gathering insights that you can actually act upon. If you have ever used any version of a popular employee engagement survey, you know where they fall short. Typical employee engagement surveys include questions like:

I have a good working relationship with my manager

I have a friend at work

I intend to stay with the organization

I would recommend the company to a family or friend

Engagement surveys tend to be eight to twelve questions like the above. What do you do with this if you get negative responses? Do you have anything *material* to react to? Engagement measures are good in the sense that it's definitely good to know how your employees feel! It's just that engagement measures fall short of being able to provide you with material insights to you can make business improvements.

We have spent years developing and refining an employee survey that functions as a business and organizational diagnostic. Of course, we would love for you to use ours, but there are others on the market to select from too. We want to encourage you to go deeper than asking your employees how they feel. Your employees have tremendous insights that they have learned through experience with your customers, each other, and everything you produce. A well-designed organizational diagnostic is vitally important as a tool which will allow you to regularly measure organizational health. The best will give you a view of all 7 disciplines. Business performance improvement is generated through a mix of all 7 disciplines; results get better when processes are smoother, people are empowered, incentives are aligned, and the organization structure enables success. When all this is done…then…engagement goes up!

11. Change Management Guidance

Chapter Focus

This chapter reviews the most common change management considerations when adjusting decision rights in an organization. It examines interdependencies with other performance disciplines, power shifts, communication needs, and position turnover.

Driving for improved decision effectiveness has organizational implications that cannot be avoided. Not addressing these implications will contribute to a failure-rate *not* a success-rate. Addressing them will help you achieve higher levels of success, and it's healthy for your business.

Interdependencies

Changing decision rights impacts other things in your organization. This fact is inescapable. Moving roles and responsibilities around may impact any or all of the other six performance disciplines. Refer to Figure 29 as we review impacts to each discipline.

Organizational Structure: Moving roles and responsibilities around on key decisions may have structural implications. Ask yourself and your leadership team these questions:

*Does the structure support the manner in which
the decision needs to be made?*

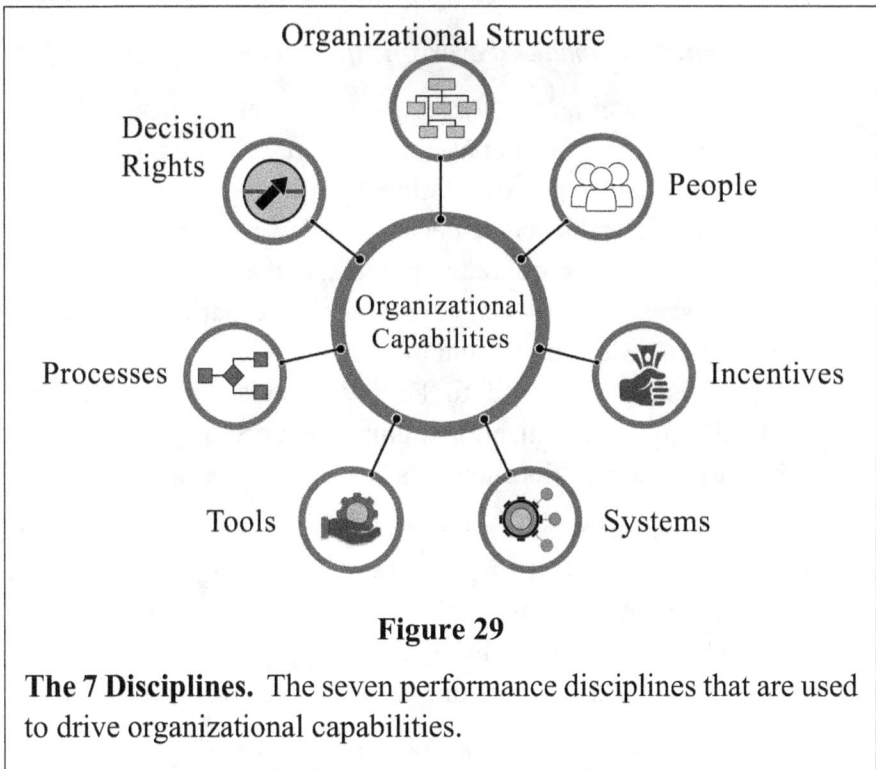

Figure 29

The 7 Disciplines. The seven performance disciplines that are used to drive organizational capabilities.

It is common to encounter a situation where the leadership team needs to select a role to fulfill the responsibility of Recommender, but a position doesn't exist in the organization that is neutral-enough or unbiased-enough to instill confidence. Assigning it to an existing position raises concerns about whether they will vet recommendations in their own interests, or in the best interests of the entire business. The leadership team will need to work through the best way to address this. Roles *can* be added or moved around in the organization, but this usually carries an addition to operational expenditures. Roles can be assigned, regardless of the bias, but this has a potential cost to decision quality, speed, and effort. It's a balancing act between costs and benefit, where intentional debate is needed among the leadership team.

Have you included everyone that has material input?

It is also common to "forget" to do a scan to ensure that all necessary organizational units are involved in the recommendation process; failure to identify all needed inputs can result in stalls and re-decision. If an important part of the organization is left out of the process, and a decision is made, it makes sense that the organization will experience a stalling while new requirements and information are considered. Then, the decision will need to be reviewed a subsequent time. Identifying all organizational units that need to participate can help avoid these "fits and starts."

Processes: We've spent quite a lot of "real estate" reviewing decision effectiveness in the context of processes. Regarding processes, one very important point to reiterate is that you are not only adjusting decision rights, you are adjusting decision *methods*. Here are some questions to consider when adjusting decision methods and rights.

Are the decisions in the workflow receiving an optimal decision method?

Remember, there are five decision methods: *Solo, Inform, Discuss, Recommend,* and *Consensus*. All five are valid methods when applied in the proper context. You may need to move key decisions to group methods using the *recommend* method (or less commonly the *consensus* method.) You may also need to move some decisions to more individualistic methods using either *solo, inform,* or *discuss*. Consider the business' need for quality, speed, and effort in the selection of the method.

For those "key" decisions requiring a group process, have we modified the process workflow to explicitly address the recommendation?

As shown in Figure 22 in an earlier chapter, it is highly useful to make the recommendation and communications steps explicit in the process workflow. This ensures that the entire team understands the increase in formality and importance of a decision.

> *For those "key" decisions requiring a group process, have you modified the acronym used in the responsibility matrix to reflect the new roles?*

There are several acronyms that can be used for coding roles in a responsibility matrix. RACI/RASCI could certainly be continued through the recommendation and decision steps in a process workflow; however, the passivity of the consult and inform coding is not ideal. Using a RAPIDS codding is markedly better.

People: When decision methods and/or rights are adjusted, there will be impacts *to* people and dependencies *on* people. The role and positional adjustments are part of the organizational discipline. In the people discipline you'll need to address, at a minimum, the following questions:

> *Do the people have the knowledge and skills to effectively perform their new roles?*

There is a minimum of three areas to consider for knowledge and skills.

1) Ensure that everyone is versed in decision effectiveness and its impact on business performance; all should be aware of the interdependencies with processes, organizational structure, systems, tools, people, and incentives.
2) Ensure that everyone understands what success looks like for the role(s) they're fulfilling (e.g. What's a

good *material* and *active* input look like? What makes a good recommendation?)

3) Ensure that everyone has the technical/job knowledge necessary for effective performance in their role(s).

Do we have the right people in the right roles?

This is an on-going examination for all businesses, but it becomes pronounced when changes are made to decision methods and rights. You may need to move people around to play to the team's strengths and maximize effectiveness.

Do we have talent gaps that we need to fill?

This is also an on-going examination for all businesses. Changes in decision methods and rights can present specific talent needs that will have to be filled in order to achieve higher levels of effectiveness. This could also be an organizational design issue, or it may be an issue with open positions that need to be filled. Changes in decisioning will amplify these needs.

Incentives: Behavior follows rewards and incentives. Keep in mind that incentives do not have to be monetary. They could be social recognition, professional recognition, opportunity to develop, and a myriad of other variations. Also keep in mind that incentives are not just a people consideration, which is why it's called out as its own discipline; businesses also incentivize across supply chains, both upstream and downstream. It's not uncommon to make changes in decision methods and rights that require supply chain partner involvement. We don't want to rule out the monetary aspect, quite the contrary, incentives can include the potential for monetary gains for your team members and supply chain partners. The following are good questions to ask around incentives:

*Have the changes in decision methods/rights also
changed compensable factors?*

In the realm of incentives and compensation, there are things
known as "compensable factors." A compensable factor is a
material element of a job that determines its market-value.
These factors are bundled together, rated and weighed, and then
used to establish pay bands and target compensation levels.
Compensable factors are written from the perspective of the
position and what is minimally required to successfully execute
the duties of the position. A typical set of compensable factors
include education, experience, job complexity, decision
responsibility/authority, impact of decisions on the company,
supervision scope, sensitivity to intellectual property, and
working conditions. The addition of decision responsibility,
authority, and autonomy can increase the incentive targets of a
position when compared to market. Conversely, the removal of
decision responsibility, authority, and autonomy can decrease
the incentive targets of a position compared to market. A
compensation review should be conducted for any substantial
changes in role and authority level.

*Have the changes in decision methods/rights also
changed involvement from supply chain partners
which require incentive review?*

If changes in decision method, (likely a move toward group
methods) necessitates increased involvement from your supply
chain partners, (likely providing input or follow-on execution,)
you may need to reexamine how you incentivize. Increased
work expectations can result in a need to revisit service level
agreements and contract terms. Consequently, remuneration
may also need to be considered if the increase in expectation is
material to the supplier.

Systems: Systems impact from changing decision methods and rights is unavoidable in most companies. At one level or another, our companies rely on systems for the movement and processing of work. Here are a couple questions that will help guide your review of systemization:

> *Have we changed authority levels of positions that need to be reflected in our operational systems?*

For example, if you change a position's level of authority for purchasing, that change probably needs to be reflected in a system. A common point of reference for systems are "tables of authority." Any workflow with decision changes, that also has system-enabled workflow-automation, should be reviewed.

> *Would any of the changes in decision rights benefit from additional systemization?*

From an opposite perspective, desired changes in decision methods/rights may lend itself to systemization. It may be beneficial to put in place additional automation and systemization. Systemization will enforce the manner of execution and ensure that the decision authority and accountability is placed with the right role.

Tools: Having the right job tools is one of the most overlooked of the seven performance disciplines. We are so tool-rich in our modern workplace that our instinct is to assume we have what we need. That's often not the case. One tool that is missing almost all the time is a template for presenting recommendations. When addressing key decisions that require a group method, most often the *recommend* method, companies lack an agreed-upon template for how a recommendation should be made. The toolkit that we use has these templates pre-built for ready-application. That's just one example; tools of all types may be needed. Here are some questions to help you review the need:

Do the right people have the assessment tools
they need to properly diagnose the situation and
perform their decision roles?

Assessment tools are critical regardless of decision method applied. Group methods (*recommend* and *consensus*) can be more complex from a job tools standpoint because each member of the team needs to have proper tool access for *their* portion of the workflow. Proper tools access by each member is critical for maximum decision effectiveness. Conversely, if you moved decisions toward an individualistic method, (*solo, inform*, or *discuss*) these people also need access *and competence* with the tools to perform their roles effectively. As a matter of fact, when using individualistic methods, tools access and competence become even more critical because there's not a team backing each other up. If one individual is missing the tools and/or competence, then every decision they make will potentially suffer from quality and speed issues.

Do we need additional deployment of any physical
tools, informational tools, or software tools in
order for people to perform their decision roles?

Like the other questions for each of the seven disciplines, this is a brainstorming question. Job tools come in many shapes and sizes, and it's common that it takes a team of smart people working together to identify everything that's needed. It may be new tool acquisition, but it may also be tools that you already have that need to be reallocated or further deployed.

A simple form/chart, shown in Figure 30, can provide you with a lot of leverage when reviewing the seven disciplines for interdependencies. This is a good way to brainstorm your needs for each key decision that you're changing.

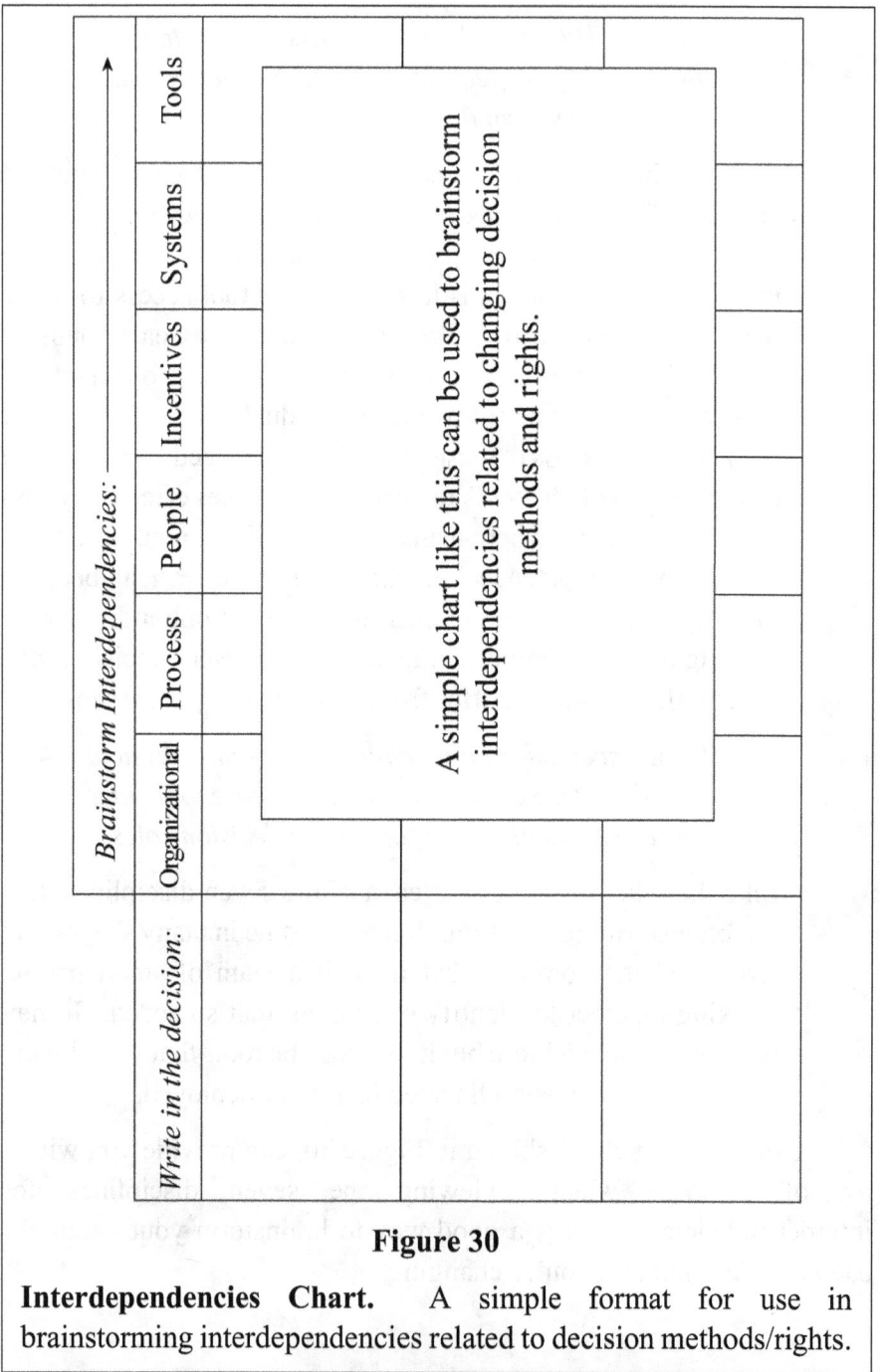

Figure 30

Interdependencies Chart. A simple format for use in brainstorming interdependencies related to decision methods/rights.

Power Changes

We reviewed power changes in a previous chapter on "Hidden Matters" because many of our organizational power structures and behaviors are unwritten. Power changes are a significant and unavoidable certainty when modifying decision methods and decision rights. The entire premise of decision effectiveness is based on establishing optimal power structures for a business (authority and autonomy.)

The first tip to navigating these power structures is to engage with transparency and work for the greater good of the organization. The purpose of doing this work is to drive improved business performance, and everyone in the company benefits from improved business performance. With all decisions, there is a need to understand the *current state*, *future state*, and what it will take to move from *current* to *future*. The best way to do this is to have the buy-in and participation of current experts and future recipients of the roles. Most people can be rationale and reasonable when approached with transparency, truth, and a cause for the betterment of all involved.

There is the very real occurrence of conflict though. Changing decision rights and methods is without a doubt an area of potential conflict, but don't be scared of it. Healthy conflict is good, but healthy conflict deals with the situation and team problem solving…it does not get personal. This is also certainly a top reason to use an external/third-party to facilitate your team. A third-party facilitator can help keep everyone focused on the goals and manage the team to exhibit healthy problem-solving behaviors.

We live in the real world, right? We must acknowledge the fact that there will be times when individuals will "dig in their heels" and be uncooperative. This is especially true if they perceive an impending loss of power and a loss of significance for their role. If you have some of these occurrences, you can use these techniques to help navigate difficult conversations about loss of power and influence:

Workflow: Often, workflow can be used to help navigate conversations. An individual may lose power at one point of the workflow but still maintain significant contributions, authority, and autonomy either upstream or downstream in the same workflow.

Workload: Does the movement of power also mean a movement of workload? If so, there may be a real benefit to the person from a workload standpoint. If the change in decision rights reflects a better balance of workload for the entire team, such a change benefits everyone.

Again, we live in the real world, right? We must also acknowledge the fact that there will be cases when there is no other choice but to deal with someone who's being resistant. If all other engagement avenues have been pursued, and an individual is in-effect "defending their territory," it is incumbent on leadership to address the undesirable behaviors directly. Not doing so is a failure of leadership. Not doing so risks the future performance of your business and the effectiveness of your decision making.

Communication and Training Needs

Much of change management hinges on communications and training. This chapter is not an exhaustive treatment of change management; instead, this brief chapter highlights a few common and needed items that help to ensure success of your decision effectiveness efforts. There are three primary communication and training areas that should be considered.

1. As reviewed in an earlier chapter, decision effectiveness is the least understood of the seven performance disciplines. Our experience working the businesses shows us that less than 10% of people have any formal exposure or experience with decision effectiveness. This means that there is a need for

training. While your leadership team(s) go through the work of identifying key decisions, remapping decision rights, and fine-tuning workflows, it is advisable to provide your entire organization with some baseline training in decision effectiveness. This way, when you are ready to implement changes in decisioning, the organization will have a solid foundation and will better understand the reasons why and how they might participate going forward.

2. As you implement the future state of workflows and decision rights, it is imperative that the changing of decision rights be formally **communicated**. Use judgement regarding the extent of the communication. A good first-start would be to ensure, at a minimum, that affected stakeholders and workflow participants are aware of any changes. Also include the rationale for the changes and the expected benefits to the business.

3. As Deciders make their choices regarding a course of action, they need to **communicate *their* decision choices** to stakeholders. The highlight here is that it is incumbent on the *Decider to communicate* (not anyone else on a team.) Often Deciders, especially executive-deciders, will delegate communications, but in the case of key decisions it is important for organizational alignment that the *Decider OWNS* their choice. If you have been entrusted with both the authority and autonomy to make a key choice on behalf of your business, it is also your responsibility to own and communicate *your choice* as *yours*. Delegating the *communication* of your choices *can appear* as abdication and an avoidance of

accountability. Abdication and avoidance of accountability is bad for your culture; don't do it. Step up. Own it. Communicate it. Completing the decision-communication is one of the strengths of the *Sustain* role in RAPIDS. The person assigned to the *Sustain* role can be very helpful to a *Decider* by facilitating the communications process.

Position Turn-Over

Turn-over of staff is a fact of business life. Optimistically, we can strive for planned and voluntary turn-over for things like promotions and rotational development. Unfortunately, we also know that unplanned turn-over occurs for reasons such as competitive offers and performance issues. It's best to plan for turn-over, and in the context of decision effectiveness this means a few things:

1. First, when selecting decision methods and mapping decision rights, ensure that you use *roles* versus people's names. This guidance was presented earlier, but it's important to re-emphasize. When we use roles, the responsibilities, authority, and autonomy stay with the *role* regardless of the person who occupies it. The decisional responsibilities should be part of a job description, and people should be selected for their ability to perform the role effectively.

2. Second, don't assume competency in decision effectiveness. Again, less than 10% of employees have formal exposure or experience in decision effectiveness. Plan for an orientation and training of all new hires who have a significant role in decision effectiveness. Best practice is to train everyone. This is why we make available an e-learning solution to our

customers. It allows them to train many employees quickly and efficiently across geographic boundaries.

3. Third, use document repositories. Collaboration tools are plentiful in today's modern business. Use these to manage decision matrices, process workflows, and other supporting collateral. Ensure that they are version controlled and accessible to the organization. This eases on-boarding of new talent and it can help to ensure overall organizational adoption.

The change management of improvements in decisioning are as important as the adjustments to decision methods and rights. Without change management, organizational adoption will suffer. Interdependencies must be solved, changes communicated, and the organization must be trained to be successful.

12. Conclusion & Summary

Decision effectiveness is a powerful discipline. Like each of the seven performance disciplines, it correlates slightly positively to improved performance. When the disciplines are used together, in the right mix, their effects are accretive. Using them together, you can be much more confident that you'll be able to achieve the performance improvements you desire in your business.

Decision effectiveness is also the one discipline that seems to be a "best kept secret." Oh, not intentionally, but maybe because it has its basis in the "soft-science" of psychology. Our businesses are comprised of people; therefore, understanding human psychology can help us all work together more effectively. The discipline of decision-making is one that very few of us have formal exposure to, and that's what makes it a bit of a secret. It's our hope that this secret discipline can be better used through education and exposure in very practical ways.

Decisioning impacts your organizational culture in dramatic ways. Ways that often go unmeasured (but can be measured.) The dimensions of authority and accountability, when intentionally and properly applied generate empowerment, trust, and forward progress. When decisioning is left to evolve and ebb and flow on its own, you can end up with negative impacts on your organizational culture. Things like employee disengagement, stalled and wasted efforts, too many initiatives, lack of alignment, high frustration, slow execution, and seemingly endless loops of indecision and redecision will occur. The only way to achieve empowerment and trust is by being intentional about decisions, roles, authorities, and accountabilities.

Effective decision making relies heavily on role clarity. To achieve optimal outcomes in decision quality, speed, yield, and effort you must first start with role and responsibility definitions. This requires a formal effort to identify key business decisions and how they *need* to work for your business. Not every decision needs to be a team effort though. It's okay to place decisions into the other methods such as *Solo, Inform,* or *Discuss*, recognizing when the business performance is better served through higher degrees of individual autonomy…the point being that as a leadership team you've looked at it and done so intentionally. On the other end of the spectrum, there are decisions which require group level involvement and will invoke the *consensus* method. This method benefits from the rigor of both process design and decision design. However, most of the *key* business decisions will be well-suited for the *recommend* method. Role clarity helps your organization render decisions both effectively and efficiently and enables you to do so over time and with consistency.

Decisioning is always performed within the context of the business ecosystem, and driving improved decision effectiveness requires learning, investment, and practice. Over 90% of employees have no formal experience or training in decision effectiveness. This high inexperience level makes decision effectiveness one of the least used performance disciplines. It also makes it one of the most impactful to business performance improvement.

Decision effectiveness does not exist alone. Using a multi-disciplinary approach ensures much higher success rates for your business initiatives. When the seven performance disciplines are combined together in the right mix, they are a *powerful* enabler of success! Decision effectiveness is a great compliment to your performance improvement efforts.

Selecting a Consulting Firm

Decision effectiveness and decision rights, performed within the context of the business ecosystem, requires practice. Decision effectiveness is *often* best used with organizational design and process design to achieve the highest success rates. The other disciplines of people, systems, tools, and incentives should be considered and used to maximize business improvement. Using a multi-disciplinary approach ensures success, and selecting a consulting firm that can guide, facilitate, and educate your leadership team is critical.

A real challenge for most companies is that they do not have dedicated practitioners in the decision effectiveness space. This challenge is made even more difficult by the dispersion of expertise that may be in place with some of the other disciplines. Your company may have people with expertise in organizational design, but those same people probably don't have experience with decision effectiveness and may not have experience with process redesign either. You're likely have expertise in systems and tools, but similarly these people probably lack exposure to decision effectiveness. There may also be sensitivities to the types of decisions that your leadership team needs to work through, and along with those sensitivities comes the potential for destructive conflict. Consequently, having an internal resource facilitate this process could have negative cultural implications.

You need people, maybe a consulting firm, with extensive skills to wield all 7 disciplines and bring them to bear on your business needs. Decision Effectiveness, along with the other six disciplines, needs to be applied at the right level, the right time, and sequenced/connected properly to drive the desired change and the greatest adoption.

The importance of a **holistic systems view** cannot be understated. As illustrated previously in Figures 32 and 33, a decision effectiveness need is most often accompanied by other needs. Rarely are business issues solved exclusively through *only* one of the seven disciplines. When selecting a consulting firm to perform any of the seven disciplines, you will be best-served to ensure that the firm has a professional vantage point rooted in systems thinking. Even when you have determined that you *only need one* of the disciplines (which is really rare), and that you're managing the rest through other means, the consulting firm should be fully-mindful of their impact to the business ecosystem and other work streams. Being able to collaborate within your business is as important as the ability to perform the technical nature of the respective discipline. After all, it is the performance of your *entire business ecosystem* that's on the line. Maximizing the benefits to the business requires full engagement and partnership.

At Alonos®, every one of our performance consultants is fully versed in systems thinking and the application of the 7 performance disciplines so that our clients gain maximum value and success from each engagement. Additionally, we use diagnostic tools/surveys that we have developed that allow you to identify and define areas in your business where there are improvement opportunities. We believe that the systems thinking approach and the 7 disciplines are the proven way to maximize results.

In our opinion, the firms you want to work with are those that are focused on *your* **capability-building**. An external consulting firm should have *your* capabilities in mind with everything they do. At our firm, we believe in business-building! It is our mission to build capabilities into our client's businesses and people. We have had consistent success by building project teams using a combination of internal and external resources. External subject matter experts/practitioners are partnered with internal resources; this enables a rapid initiation, controls costs, and helps to ensure knowledge transfer.

In our opinion, **temporary engagements** should be the *rule* when it comes to consulting. Consulting is different than outsourcing. There are many firms that are not really interested in being a consultant to you; instead, they are interested in being an outsourcer. Consultants come in, help you build capability, and leave you in a position where you can run and operate that capability on your own. If an external firm desires to perform a set of services for you on a regular, consistent, and day-to-day basis, they are an outsourcer.

Get a **good mix.** Our firm is intentional about who we partner with and employ. We select practitioners who have a mix of experience across industries and practice areas. We provide people who have deep expertise in multiple disciplines along with the education and credentials to support on-going development of the disciplines and their respective bodies of knowledge. We develop our people toward this goal: to be practitioners in all seven performance disciplines. Consequently, we are in a unique position to help you build business capabilities.

Reach out to us today:

alonos.com

information@alonos.com

References

Aggarwal, R.K., & Samwick, A.A. (2006). Empire-builders and shirkers: Investment, firm performance, and managerial incentives. *Journal of Corporate Finance 12* (2006), 489-515.

Albrecht, D.J. (2018). *Organizational Design that Sticks! Multidisciplinary approach for the business ecosystem.* Dallas, TX: Alonos Corporation.

Andersen, J.A., & Jonsson, P. (2006). Does organization structure matter?: On the relationship between structure, functioning and effectiveness. *International Journal of Innovation and Technology Management, 3*(2), (237-263). doi: 10/1142/S0219877006000788

Ashkenas, R. (2013). *Change Management Needs to Change.* Harvard Business Review. (April 16).

Barnard, C. (1948). *The functions of the executive.* Cambridge, MA: Harvard University Press.

Blenko, M.W., Mankins, M.C., & Rogers, P. (2010). *Decide & Deliver: 5 steps to breakthrough performance in your organization.* Boston, MA: Harvard Business Review Press.

Bodell, L. (2012). *5 Ways Process is Killing Your Productivity* (May 15, 2012). Fast Company. Retrieved on March 2020 from https://www.fastcompany.com/1837301/5-ways-process-killing-your-productivity

Bushman, R.M., Dai, Z., & Zhang, W. (2016). Management Team Incentive: Dispersion and firm performance. *The Accounting Review 91* (1), 21-45. doi: 10.2308/accr-51112

Carmeli, A., Sheaffer, Z., & Halevi, M.Y. (2008). Does participatory decision-making in top management teams enhance decision effectiveness and firm performance? *Personnel Review, 38*(6), (696-714). doi: 10.1108/00483480910992283

Carpenter, G. (2013). *The Second-Mover Advantage.* Kellogg Insight. Kellogg School of Management, Northwestern University. Retrieved from: https://insight.kellogg.northwestern.edu/ article/the_second_mover_advantage

Cohen, S.A., Kulp, S., & Randall, T. (2007). Motivating Supply Chain Behavior: The right incentives can make all the difference. *Supply Chain Management Review 11* (4), 18–24.

Coulson-Thomas, C. (2005). Using Job Support tools to Increase Workgroup Performance. *International Journal of Productivity and Performance Management, 54*(3), 206-211.

DePass, D. (2016). *Select Comfort's second quarter beats earnings expectations but misses on sales: Bedmaker still feeling impact from ERP computer installation.* (July 20, 2016). Star Tribune. Retrieved November 2017 from: http://www.startribune.com/select-comfort-s-2q-beats-profit-expectations-but-misses-on-sales/387702561/

Drucker, P. (1967). *The Effective Decision.* Harvard Business Review. Retrieved from: https://hbr.org/1967/01/the-effective-decision

Drucker, P. (1993). *Concept of the corporation.* London, U.K.: Transaction Publishers.

Dunn & Bradstreet. (2013). *D&B Global & U.S. Business Data.* (DB-3662 11/13). Retrieved November 2017 from: http://www.dnb.com/content/dam/english/dnb-data-insight/global-data-collection/dnb_global_and_us_business_data.pdf

Eblanna, S., & Child, J. (2007). Influences on Strategic Decision Effectiveness: Development and test of an integrative model. *Strategic Management Journal, 28*, 431-453. doi: 10/1002/smj.597

Fadhilah, A.N., & Subriadi, A.P. (2019). The Role of IT on Firm Performance. *The Fifth Information Systems International Conference 2019. Elsevier B.V.* Retrieved from http://creativecommons.org/licenses/by-nc-nd/4.0/

Garvin, D.A. (1987). *Competing on the Eight Dimensions of Quality.* Harvard Business Review. Retrieved from: https://hbr.org/1987/11/competing-on-the-eight-dimensions-of-quality

Gleeson, B. (2012). *4 Ways for Leaders to Make a Decision.* (November 7, 2012). Forbes. Retrieved on March 2020 from https://www.forbes.com/sites/brentgleeson/2012/11/07/4-ways-for-leaders-to-make-a-decision/#125f92b4d4a1

Gleeson, B. (2016). *4 Reasons Process is Destroying Your Company's Productivity* (December 2, 2016). Forbes. Retrieved on March 2020 from https://www.forbes.com/sites/brentgleeson/2016/12/02/4-reasons-process-is-destroying-your-companys-productivity/#618a95e49a1d

Guo, K., PhD, MHP. (2008) DECIDE: A decision-making model for more effective decision making by health care managers. *Health Care Management, 27*(2), 118-127. doi: 10.1097/01.HCM.0000285046.27290.90

Guttman, J., Psy.D. (2019). *Decision-Making: Facing the challenge of making 35,000 a day.* Psychology Today. Retrieved on March 2020 from https://www.psychologytoday.com/us/blog/sustainable-life-satisfaction/201907/decision-making-facing-the-challenge-making-35000-day

Henning, R. (2010). Shop Management Tools Speed Job-Shop Performance and Productivity. *Manufacturing Engineering* (145)6. 22-24.

Kahneman, D. (2011). *Thinking, Fast and Slow.* New York, NY: Farrar, Straus and Giroux.

Kanaracus, C. (2013). *Senate to probe failed Air Force ERP software project.* (January 25, 2013). Computerworld. Retrieved November 2017 from: https://www.computerworld.com/article/2494760/vertical-it/senate-to-probe-failed-air-force-erp-software-project.html

Kim, H.J. (2017). Information Technology and Firm Performance: The role of supply chain integration, *Springer Science and Business Media Operations Management, 10,* 1-9. doi: 10.1007/s12063-016-0122-z

Larson, E. (2018). *New Research: The 7 decision practices top companies use to innovate.* Forbes. (Oct 8, 2018) Retrieved from: https://www.forbes.com/sites/eriklarson/2018/10/08/new-research-the-7-decision-practices-top-companies-use-to-innovate-and-win/#6e93bb7f53e7

Loshali, S., & Krishnan, V.R. (2013). Strategic Human Resource Management and Firm Performance: Mediating role of transformational leadership. *Journal of Strategic Human Resource Management, 2* (1). 9-19.

Mahalawat, V., & Sharma, B. (2018). Correlation between Business Process Management and Organizational Performance: A study of Bank X. *International Journal of Engineering and Management Research, 8* (2). doi: doi.org/10/31033/ijemr.v8i02.11864

Nourayi, M.M., & Krishnan, S. (2006). The Impact of Incentives on CEO Compensation and Firm Performance. *Rivista Internazionale di Scienze Economiche e Commerciali 53.3* (2006): 402–420.

Porter, M.E. (1998). *Competitive Advantage: Creating and sustaining superior performance.* New York, NY: The Free Press.

Regis, T., & Krause, D.R. (2015). Competition or Cooperation? Promoting supplier performance with incentives under varying conditions of dependence. *Journal of Supply Chain Management, 51* (4). 29-53.

Sashkin, M., & Sashkin, M.G. (2003). *Leadership that Matters: The critical factors for making a difference in people's lives and organizations' success.* San Francisco, CA: Berrett-Koehler Publishers, Inc.

Senge, P.M. (2006). *The fifth discipline: The art & practice of the learning organization.* New York, NY: Doubleday.

Sheng, Y.P. & Mykytyn, P.P. (2002). Information Technology Investment and Firm Performance: A perspective of data quality. *Proceedings of the Seventh International Conference on Information Quality (ICIQ-02),* 132-141.

Singh, A. (2009). Organizational Power in Perspective. *Leadership and Management in Engineering, 9* (4), doi: https://doi.org/10.1061/(ASCE)LM.1943-5630.0000018

Skarzauskiene, A. (2010). Managing complexity: systems thinking as a catalyst of the organizational performance. *Measuring Business Excellence, 14*(4), 49-64. doi: 10.1108/13683041011093758

Sujova, A., Marcinekova, K., & Simanova, L. (2019). Influence of Modern Process Performance Indicators on Corporate Performance – the Empirical Study. *Engineering Management in Production and Services 11* (2), 119-129. doi: 10.2478/emj-2019-0015

Thibodeau, P. (2017). *MillerCoors seeks $100M in damages from IT contractor.* (March 21, 2017). Computerworld. Retrieved November 2017 from: https://www.computerworld.com/article/3183470/it-outsourcing/millercoors-seeks-100m-in-damages-from-it-contractor.html

Vroom, V.H., & Yetton, P.W. (1973). *Leadership and Decision-Making.* London, UK: Feffer and Simons, Inc.

Wright, P.M., Gardner, T.M., Moyhnihan, L.M., & Allen, M.R. (2005). The Relationship Between HR Practices and Firm Performance: Examining causal order. *Personnel Psychology*, (58). 409-446

Wyngaard, C.J., Pretorius, J.H., & Pretorius, L. (2012). *Theory of the Triple Contraint: A conceptual review (December 2012, IEEE IEEM Conference Paper.)* Retrieved March 2020 from https://www.researchgate.net/publication/271455172 | doi: 10.1109/IEEM.2012.6838095

Yanadori, Y., & Cui, V. (2013). Creating Incentives for Innovation: The relationship between pay dispersion in R&D groups and firm innovation performance. *Strategic Management Journal 34* (March), 1502-1511.

Index

accountability	37, 38, 39, 41, 83, 105, 123, 148, 154
authority	31, 37, 38, 39, 41, 52, 58, 59, 62, 76, 81, 82, 83, 116, 147, 148, 151, 152, 153, 154
benchmark	140
brittle	22, 26
bureaucracy	76
business leadership	39
capabilities	27, 160, 161
CEO	x, 29, 30
clarity	38, 47, 50, 51, 52, 53, 55, 56, 84, 86, 102, 103, 105, 113, 115, 126
coercion	58
communications	36, 152, 153
conflict of interest	30
consensus	83, 86, 92, 94, 97, 123, 144
correlation	27, 33, 35, 36, 40, 41, 48, 66, 67, 68
cultural	36
culture	21, 36, 36, 38, 40, 100, 154
DECIDE	83, 106, 107, 126, 145, 164
decision effectiveness	26, 36, 40, 41, 47, 51, 56, 62-63, 65, 116, 131, 152, 154, 157
decision making	35, 36, 38, 39, 40, 42, 50, 52, 55, 58, 78, 81, 82, 83, 84, 86, 89, 96, 106, 116, 118, 119, 126, 131, 152, 164
decision rights	31, 42, 52, 53, 55, 77, 83, 103, 105, 113, 116, 117, 123, 126, 130, 142, 144, 148, 151, 152, 153, 154
decision tree	83, 84, 86, 98
decisioning	31, 99, 157

www.ingramcontent.com/pod-product-compliance
Lightning Source LLC
Chambersburg PA
CBHW050524270326
41926CB00015B/3064